*An* ~

# EMPOWERED BY GOD

## ANOINTED FOR ACTION

*Expect More See More!*
*Eph. 3:20-21*

## BOBBY CONNER

### EAGLES VIEW MINISTRIES

# AUTHOR PROFILE

Bobby and Carolyn Conner are founder and President of Eagles View Ministries (EVM), a global outreach that focuses on revealing a demonstration of God's power—"Empowering the Body of Christ to Take Dominion." Their goal is to prepare an overcoming generation that transcends gender and age, raising the standard of purity and power in order to transform nations. Sounding the alarm, they are awakening the warriors to arise and contend for the true faith, advancing the King in His Kingdom.

Bobby and Carolyn Conner have been married for forty-eight years. They have two sons and two wonderful daughters-in-love, as well as four grandchildren. They pastored Southern Baptist churches for twenty-seven years, and they have been ministering for almost five decades in over fifty nations across the earth!

They are passionate and inspired by a global vision for establishing the Kingdom of God in a true demonstration of God's power, knowing that the Kingdom does not consist of mere words, but of Holy Spirited–empowered works (see 1 Cor. 4:20). Bobby and Carolyn are on a mission to fulfill the Kingdom-empowerment mandate of Heaven. Bobby has authored numerous books, and he has averaged speaking five times a week for over four decades; together, they have a burning passion to spread the uncompromised message of the Kingdom of God to every nation.

You can discover more about their ministry at:

www.bobbyconner.org.

# CONTENTS

# INTRODUCTION

A s followers of Christ Jesus, we are expected to accomplish the same supernatural works He did and even greater. This statement seems absolutely unbelievable until we discover its source—the Lord Jesus Christ (see John 14:12). The standard has been set high; with such a task before us, we are compelled to seek divine empowerment. Because we are called and commissioned to walk in Kingdom authority and power (see Luke 10:19), we are challenged to seek deeper intimacy with the Holy Spirit, who will equip us to live empowered Kingdom lives. If we permit Him, the Holy Spirit will motivate and transform us into empowered and enlightened people (see Acts 1:8). The Scriptures lay the foundation for our answer to the age-old question: What am I born to accomplish, and can I truly live an empowered life?

As believers, our core goal and main mission in life is to live lifestyles inspired and directed by God's Word as a blueprint to accomplish God's vision and destiny for our lives. With that in mind, we must make up our minds that we are going to be history-makers. We can do incredible things with His help!

As you journey through the pages of this book, expect to be instructed on how to position yourself to gain valuable insights in Kingdom dominion and true authority. You will discover that the Word of God is a sure and stable foundation (see Ps. 119:89). Discovering the power of proclamation, you will realize how to execute the spoken Word in order to live a victorious and God-empowered life. By this, you will acquire the keys to overcoming the painful failures of the past, putting them behind you and looking ahead, ready to conquer every obstacle that the foe puts in your path. You will be challenged not to permit the failures of the past to keep you from enjoying the victories of your future (see Jer. 31:17).

Likewise, your spirit will be invigorated to pursue the presence of the King. In His presence, the fullness of joy abides (see Ps. 16:11). As you reside in His presence, God will prepare you to pursue personal, corporate, and global dreams and goals. The truth is, you are called to be a history-maker and a world-changer! Never forget the fact that a passionate few can direct the entire course of nations.

This book will also aid you in realizing how to embrace the process and purpose of spiritual character and maturity, and it will highlight to you the importance of investing your life into the Kingdom. You will grasp insights that will teach you how to be steadfast, divinely stubborn, and persistent, never giving up on God's vision and purpose for your life. You must be steadfast and unstoppable in your journey to divine empowerment (see 1 Cor. 15:58). It is time to exit the pathway of apathy and to advance in the journey to divine empowerment so that you may become a spiritual revolutionary who is ready to shape the future!

# CHAPTER 1
## *God Has Empowered You*

L et's say it out loud right now: "I have a God-given purpose!" We were chosen by Almighty God in eternity *past* to live in the *present* in order to forge the *future* (see Eph. 2:10). We have divine destiny. No one on earth can accomplish what each of us—individually—have been commissioned to do. It's time for the Church as a whole to understand God's opinion of us: We are essential to His eternal plans and purposes! We must allow that identity to define us so that we can become the bold, brave, and radiant warriors we are called to be. Let us arise, lift our heads high, square our shoulders, and walk with confidence and assurance that God is with us everywhere we go. Therefore, we will be radiant and shine brightly in this sin-darkened world.

Not long ago, I had a strong prophetic encounter that applies to all of us. I was sound asleep when I was awakened by an exceptionally pleasant voice speaking in my room. The message was articulated with extreme clarity. As I heard the words, immense comfort and courage immediately flooded my heart. This word was audible; it was not something I heard in my head or heart, but with my ears.

However, let me be straightforward. I did not see who spoke to me because, when I looked in the direction of the voice, I was suddenly blinded by a bright flash of light. It was almost as if a strong flash from a camera had blinded my eyes. Yet, the voice continued to speak, saying, "Tell My people they have purpose—they have been chosen by Me for Me." As I heard this declaration, I was immediately overwhelmed with joy and excitement. This truth can keep us from ever allowing the devil to discourage us again; we have divine purpose!

Each one of us is divinely prepared to accomplish the task God has assigned to us. Each of us can do something that no other human being can do. We must meditate on and ponder this message until we truly believe that we have been chosen by Christ for Christ and our lives will take on even greater zeal and purpose. Jesus said:

> You did not choose Me, but I chose you and appointed you that you should go and bear fruit, and that your fruit should remain, that whatever you ask the Father in My name He may give you (John 15:16).

Our confidence and courage will soar as we begin to understand in greater capacity the depth of these words—we are chosen by Christ! May these words wash over our souls—they are like refreshing water to the thirsty. I cannot say it too many times. We have been chosen by Christ, for Christ; the choice was made before the foundation of the world (see Eph. 1:4). When we really get this promise, we will find freedom from all rejection and depression.

## THE SPIRIT OF EVANGELISM

Our goal in this life is to finish the course and to be able to say with all confidence, "I've kept the faith and stayed on course, accomplishing the task set before me" (see 2 Tim. 4:7).

To such faithful individuals, Christ will say, *"Well done, good and faithful servant..."* (Matt. 25:21). When we understand this, we will live purposefully, using all that God has given us in order to make an impact for the Kingdom. God gives us His power for a purpose; the gifts are tools, not toys, and the anointing is for action (see Acts 1:8). God releases His anointing on His children for one main purpose—to impact the nations and to bring the hurting and lost to Himself.

Recently, while I was ministering in a large arena, I saw what appeared to be a silver flowing river of light above the heads of the people. This beautiful river flowed for a short moment and then disappeared. I asked, "Lord, what is that?"

He quickly replied, "I am releasing a spirit of evangelism upon the earth."

When I heard this, I simply stated to the crowd in that arena, "God is releasing a spirit of evangelism!" The moment those words came from my mouth, nine people jumped to their feet, ran forward, fell on their knees, repented, and gave their lives to Christ Jesus, receiving Him as their personal Savior. No one was giving an altar call; these people simply responded in a burst of the Holy Spirit. To me, it was a sign that we are being summoned to the harvest field. God wants all people to be saved and to come to know Christ Jesus as both Savior and Lord (see 1 Tim. 2:4).

## POWER-HUNGRY FOR THE RIGHT REASONS

Recently, the Lord spoke an incredibly encouraging word to me, saying, "My people are becoming power-hungry for all the right reasons!" The first step to becoming anointed for action is to nurture a deep, driving hunger for change; we must become fed-up with business as usual in the Church. This is a season of sensitivity, and if we seek Him, we will find the Lord in a much deeper and more intimate way (see

Jer. 29:12-13). The Spirit of God has been fanning the flame of discontentment within the hearts of His people, creating an insatiable hunger to see the power of God revealed so that we will not settle for less than He desires to give us (see Ps. 90:16-17). The discontentment is driving us to seek the Lord and to search for His answers to life's problems (see Ps. 42:1-2; 63:1-3).

The Spirit of Truth is preparing us for spiritual promotion. We each have a divine destiny, and we are called to be powerful conduits for change. We are anointed to be history-makers and culture-changers. Let's make up our minds that we are going to make a difference; like Daniel, let's commit our whole hearts to God, deciding to live pure and clean lives, even in the midst of a culture that celebrates sin and shame (see Dan. 1:8).

## THE KING'S CHARIOT

During a recent powerful prophetic experience, a mighty messenger from Heaven visited me. Mere words are too weak to accurately explain how it all unfolded, but I will attempt to convey it because it holds significance for us all. I was sitting in the shelter of my front porch in Moravian Falls, North Carolina, on a cloudy, rainy day. Suddenly, I heard what sounded like a jet airplane flying extremely low toward my house. The sound was very loud and was approaching incredibly fast. I rushed quickly to the West side of my porch, expecting to see a jet plane burst through the low hanging clouds. *What pilot in his right mind would dare fly this low in weather conditions like this?* I thought to myself.

To my shock and utter surprise, suddenly a beautiful and brilliant angel exploded through the clouds! He was enormous and breathtaking in appearance. He stood over fifty feet tall and had wings that extended over thirty feet. He was radiant—a shimmering and glowing silver, with sapphire light whirling about him. This massive and majestic angel commanded me, "Prepare the King's chariot!" Stunned, I was about to inquire for more information when suddenly he spoke again: "Prepare the chariot of the King!" Suddenly, I understood. It is time for us to recognize that we are the vehicle and vessel; within us resides the power of God. In other words, we are each the chariot of the King (see Acts 1:8).

We can be encouraged by the powerful promise of Joshua 1:9, which states: *"Have I not commanded you? Be strong and of good courage; do not be afraid, nor be dismayed, for the Lord your God is with you wherever you go."* God has commanded us to be of good courage and to be filled with confidence and boldness, totally assured that we are not alone in our tasks. Almighty God is always with us.

## THE SAME AUTHORITY

We are called and commissioned as ambassadors for Christ and ministers of reconciliation in order to share the gospel with lost people so that they can have the opportunity to be saved (see 2 Cor. 5:18-20). An *ambassador* is a senior representative who is sent forth with authority. This can seem like a daunting task, but we can glean courage and confidence from the fact that we have been given the *same* authority as the One who sent us out (see Matt. 28:18). Jesus gave us His anointing in order to empower us and enable us to carry out His Great Commission to make disciples of all the nations (see Matt. 28:18-20).

Early in His public ministry, Jesus said, regarding His mission from His Father:

> *The Spirit of the Lord is upon Me, because He has anointed Me to preach the gospel to the poor; He has*

*sent Me to heal the brokenhearted, to proclaim liberty to the captives and recovery of sight to the blind, to set at liberty those who are oppressed; to proclaim the acceptable year of the Lord* (Luke 4:18-19).

As believers and disciples of Christ, we have His Spirit dwelling inside us, and because of this, we have the same mission Jesus did. We also have His anointing. If Jesus needed the anointing of His Father in order to carry out His mission, how much more do we need it? Because of His anointing in us, we must never underestimate ourselves, knowing that God has lofty goals for us. We can be confident that God would not give us an assignment without releasing to us an anointing. He never gives us a task without also giving a divine touch to empower us and enable us to accomplish the mission.

# CHAPTER 2
## *The Kingdom Company*

Truly, we are living in the main event, and we were born for this time and this purpose (see Esther 4:14). We have been invited to participate in fulfilling the highest and most noble quest—establishing the King in His Kingdom. We are called to stand strong, becoming an empowered and invincible Kingdom Company and driving back the powers of darkness and bringing forth the Light of God. The challenge has been issued: Be bold, be brave, and be very courageous (see Josh. 1:7-9). The Spirit of God is calling forth a powerful people—the Kingdom Company. As members of this Kingdom Company, our highest goal is to establish and advance the Kingdom of God!

In a powerful prophetic encounter, the Lord instructed me, "Prepare Me a remnant to go to the next new level!" This was not a suggestion, but rather a command. We must prepare ourselves to advance forward into God's new way for God's new day (see Josh. 3:4). This is the invitation. God is releasing a Kingdom Company; will we be part of it? In another powerful prophetic encounter, I heard the Lord say: "I am releasing a Kingdom Company—an emerging generation who will take charge. Moving in authority and power, they will rule the visible world from the invisible realm." This is an incredible promise, and we are invited to participate in it!

## WHO ARE THEY?

God's Kingdom Company will consist of overcomers! Gender and age have absolutely nothing to do with it. It matters not whether we are young or old, male or female. The issue is, do we have burning hearts filled with the motivation to see the Lord Jesus establish His Kingdom on earth? This is what sets apart those who are part of the Kingdom Company. With no other agenda, their uppermost goal will be to assure that Christ Jesus receives the glory due His name. Exalting the King in His Kingdom must be our highest goal. Some of the overwhelming benefits of becoming a true overcomer are revealed in the Book of Revelation:

> *Behold, I stand at the door and knock. If anyone hears My voice and opens the door, I will come in to him and dine with him, and he with Me. To him who overcomes I will grant to sit with Me on My throne, as I also overcame and sat down with My Father on His throne. He who has an ear, let him hear what the Spirit says to the churches* (Rev. 3:20-22).

## A MORE EXCELLENT WAY—LOVE

God is calling and commissioning His Kingdom Company to function in dominion authority—revealing His sovereignty and power, yet operating from a firm foundation of Christ's love. If we want to be part of His Company, we must prepare our hearts to receive a fresh baptism of Christ's love. This emerging generation will demonstrate dominion demeanor and establish God's Kingdom with Christ-centered love. The Spirit of God is releasing the much-needed grace to display

God's love while demonstrating Kingdom authority. We have sought God's *power*, but He longs to release *passion* first. A baptism of love is being released, and it is the love of Jesus Christ that will ultimately motivate us. Remember, God's love never fails.

This Kingdom Company will move and minister from a foundation of genuine love and humility. *"But earnestly desire the best gifts. And yet I show you a more excellent way"* (1 Cor. 12:31). The more excellent way is love. We must walk the higher way, the way of true Christ-centered love. We have sought power, yet God longs to release true passion.

## THE GREATEST GIFT

Love is the key that unlocks the hardest hearts. Love covers the most dreadful sins. Love always works; it never fails. Directly following his promise to show us a *"more excellent way,"* Paul gives these insights into true Christ-type love:

*Though I speak with the tongues of men and of angels, but have not love, I have become sounding brass or a clanging cymbal.*

*And though I have the gift of prophecy, and understand all mysteries and all knowledge, and though I have all faith, so that I could remove mountains, but have not love, I am nothing.*

*And though I bestow all my goods to feed the poor, and though I give my body to be burned, but have not love, it profits me nothing.*

*Love suffers long and is kind; love does not envy; love does not parade itself, is not puffed up; does not behave rudely, does not seek its own, is not provoked, thinks no evil; does not rejoice in iniquity, but rejoices in the truth; bears all things, believes all things, hopes all things, endures all things.*

*Love never fails. But whether there are prophecies, they will fail; whether there are tongues, they will cease; whether there is knowledge, it will vanish away. For we know in part and we prophesy in part. But when that which is perfect has come, then that which is in part will be done away.*

*When I was a child, I spoke as a child, I understood as a child, I thought as a child; but when I became a man, I put away childish things. For now we see in a mirror, dimly, but then face to face. Now I know in part, but then I shall know just as I also am known.*

*And now abide faith, hope, love, these three; but the greatest of these is love* (1 Cor. 13:1-13).

The Spirit of God is releasing wonderful grace so that we can clearly learn the lessons of *love.* Nothing is as significant as genuine, Christ-centered love. Through our love for one another, all people will know and recognize that we are truly followers of Christ (see John 13:35). For this reason, our prayer should be that we would increase and abound in Christ's love: *"And may the Lord make you increase and abound in love to one another and to all, just as we do to you"* (1 Thess. 3:12). The Body of Christ is learning to love—this is the key to melting and opening the hardest hearts because *"love never fails."* Programs fail and the plans of people fail, but God's love never fails. This kind of love is not cheap, worldly sentiment; it is costly and precious. True Christ-like love will cost us everything.

God is calling for passionate people who are willing to lay down their lives and give without expecting to gain any worldly acceptance. This generation will be aglow with the glory of God because they will be marching to the rhythm of His heartbeat. His heart will be their hearts' desire. They will resolve to follow the Lamb wherever He goes, even to the ends of the earth, and they will be willing to die for what they believe. Never has the world witnessed such passion. These hearts, set ablaze by God's love, will rush into the harvest fields, which will result in raging fires of revival across the nations. Entire nations can be saved in a single day when we walk radically in His presence.

The man, Christ Jesus, is the ultimate example, for us, of God dwelling with us. The Bible says, *"And the Word became flesh, and dwelt among us, and we beheld His glory, the glory as of the only begotten of the Father, full of grace and truth"* (John 1:14). Notice the phrase *"and we beheld His glory."* This emerging Kingdom Company will have the same countenance as Jesus—the glory of the Lord will be evident upon them. He is our pattern; He alone is our true example. As Jesus walked the earth, He was the perfect demonstration of God's unfathomable love. As we fix our gaze on Him, as the perfect model of a life of love (see 2 Cor. 3:18), we too will be walking demonstrations of God's love for the world.

## BE LIKE JESUS

As followers of Christ Jesus, we are created in the image of God and are of utmost importance to Him. He is calling us to walk in perfect unity with Him—in His likeness and His nature. God is love (see 1 John 4:8), and our mission is to be the fragrance of Christ, the beauty of Jesus, the very anointing of Him on the earth. As we minister, we minister with Him. As we walk, we walk like Him. Jesus prayed to the Father:

*I pray also for those who will believe in me through their message, that all of them may be one, Father, just as you are in me and I am in you. May they also*

*be in us so that the world may believe that you have
sent me. I have given them the glory that you gave
me, that they may be one as we are one: I in them and
you in me. May they be brought to complete unity to
let the world know that you sent me and have loved
them even as you have loved me. Father, I want those
you have given me to be with me where I am, and to
see my glory, the glory you have given me because
you loved me before the creation of the world* (John
17:20-24 NIV).

It is awesome to see how the Spirit of truth is changing the
attitude of many in the Body of Christ; their motive is truly
to give, not just get. This is the true Christ-like character we
must display to a hurting world. Our goal is for our character
to mirror Christ Jesus:

*Who, being in very nature God, did not consider
equality with God something to be grasped, but made
him- self nothing, taking the very nature of a servant,
being made in human likeness. And being found
in appearance as a man, he humbled himself and
became obedient to death—even death on a cross!
Therefore God exalted him to the highest place and
gave him the name that is above every name, that at
the name of Jesus every knee should bow, in heaven
and on earth and under the earth, and every tongue
confess that Jesus Christ is Lord, to the glory of God
the Father* (Phil. 2:6-11 NIV).

Our mission and mandate from Heaven is to have the
passion and compassion to love God and to love our
neighbors. With *compassion*, Jesus embraced the man with
leprosy, held the dying women, and broke the law in order
to sit at the well and talk to a prostitute. He was driven by
compassion:

*But when He saw the multitudes, He was moved with compassion for them, because they were weary and scattered, like sheep having no shepherd. Then He said to His disciples, "The harvest truly is plentiful, but the laborers are few. Therefore, pray to the Lord of the harvest to send out laborers into His harvest"* (Matt. 9:36-38).

Truly, love is the most excellent way because love will never fail. Love is God's greatest reflection, and it covers a multitude of sins (see 1 Pet. 4:8). It is our great privilege to be an expression of God's love in this world!

Even those of us who have not walked closely with the Lord have this invitation. God longs to heal our hearts with His love so that we too can be carriers in this world. In Hosea 14:4, God promised, *"I will heal their backsliding, I will love them freely: for mine anger has turned away from him"* (KJV). Even for those who have fallen away from faith, He is always ready to offer tender loving forgiveness. Truly, as Proverbs 10:12 states, *"Love covers all sins."*

## DOMINION DEMEANOR

The Spirit of God is establishing *sons and daughters*, not mere servants. We were created in Christ Jesus to rule as Kingdom kings. It is time for the Body of Christ to move from theory to *execution* and *action*. As Scripture declares, it is the people who know their God who will display strength and take action (see Dan. 11:32). God never intended to establish His Kingdom with just mere words; He intended to establish His Kingdom with power (see 1 Cor. 4:20).

The word *dominion* speaks of "a forceful show or display of manifested power and authority," the key words being *show* and *display*. Authority that is not activated is neutralized. The word *neutralized* speaks of "being made ineffective, especially by removing the ability to act as a threat or obstacle." Another meaning is: "to make something's potential *zero*." This is the foe's intent; the devil doesn't care about our religious activity, just as long as he is effective in neutralizing our true Kingdom power.

*Demeanor* deals with behavior, manner, or appearance—especially as it reflects on character and conduct. We are called and commissioned to become Heaven's agency for Kingdom rule on earth. We are designed to embody the nature of God on earth and to serve as His divine representatives in both the physical and spiritual realms.

## TAKE IT BACK

The devil is a thief, and he will plunder our lives if we permit him to do so. We are told to first draw near to God and then to resist the devil so that he will flee (see James 4:7). As we resist him and take a stand to regain what has been stolen, we can receive even greater than what we once had. This is God's heart toward us. If we listen, we will hear Heaven shouting the promise of restoration (see Joel 2:25). One generation will receive the restoration of everything Adam lost in the Fall. This is our purpose; this is the Kingdom Company's goal.

The creation and commissioning of humanity was the first introduction and establishment of the Kingdom of Heaven on earth. God's first intent is His present purpose (see Gen.1:26). However, the entire world is in cosmic calamity because of humanity's rebellion and the subsequent neutralization of dominion authority. Now, God is looking for a people who will take their place (see 2 Chron. 16:9). Let's embrace the promise released in Exodus 19:5-6:

> *Now therefore, if you will indeed obey My voice and keep My covenant, then you shall be a special treasure*

*to Me above all people; for all the earth is Mine. And you shall be to Me a kingdom of priests and a holy nation. These are the words which you shall speak to the children of Israel.*

Obedience is a key factor in establishing the Kingdom of God. We cannot build according to our pattern; only as we trust and obey Him will true understanding be revealed. So often, there is a way that seems right, but it is the way of destruction and death (see Prov. 14:12). God's plans truly are higher and far more magnificent than human plans. Thus, the most exciting, exhilarating life we could live is a life under the direction of God (see Jer. 29:11; Isa. 55:9).

# CHAPTER 3
## *Our True Identity*

It is imperative that we realize our identity in Christ. In Colossians 2:9, we discover this central fact concerning Christ Jesus: *"For in Him dwells all the fullness of the Godhead bodily."* The next verse is revolutionary; it will change our outlook on life. *"And you are complete in Him, who is the head of all principality and power"* (Col. 2:10). We are complete, which means that we lack nothing at all as we abide in *Him!* Abiding in Christ and allowing Him to flow freely out of us enables us to function with the greatest degree of success, thus fulfilling God's call upon our lives. As the apostle John wrote, *"Love has been perfected among us in this: that we may have boldness in the Day of Judgment; because as He is, so are we in this world"* (1 John 4:17).

Understanding our true identity is essential to obtaining our divine destiny. We are being established as *Kingdom kings and priests.* We are called to success and to walk in overcoming victory, and the task set before us is no small task; we are called to restore the desolate heritages of many generations.

*Thus says the LORD: "In an **acceptable time** I have*

*heard You, and in the **day of salvation** I have helped You; I will preserve You and give You as a covenant to the people, to restore the earth, to cause them to inherit the desolate heritages" (Isa. 49:8).*

This is the acceptable time; in other words, this is the time of God's overflowing favor. This is a time when Heaven is open to our prayers. God's Spirit is saying, "I have heard you!" God's Word promises that if we ask anything according to His will, we will receive what we are asking for (see 1 John 5:14-15). According to the passage in Isaiah, this is also *"the day of salvation"*—a day to receive the help and support of the Lord (see Ps. 121:1-5). This is also the day of the restoration of desolate heritages; we can expect to recover what many generations have lost! The season we live in is an incredibly important and unique season of advancing the Kingdom of God. We are truly in His Kingdom *"for such a time as this"* (Esther 4:14). His Kingdom is in each one of us for such a time as this.

## MISSED DIAGNOSES

For this reason, we cannot afford missed diagnoses; it is time to believe the truth about who we are. Now is the time to grasp the promises of God concerning our destiny through Christ—that we are *more* than conquerors (see Rom. 8:37). Greater is the power of God within us than all the powers of evil in the world (see 1 John 4:4).

Contrary to the secular view, this world is not a *playground*, but a *battleground*. Our lives are either a series of testimonies gained from battles won or a list of regrets from past defeats. We must choose the first, and fight to maintain that in our lives at all cost. We have a mandate from Heaven to develop a militant attitude, in holy violence, to stop every advance of the devil (see Eph. 6:12-13). We must let this promise of victory arise within us: *"For whatever is born of God overcomes the world. And this is the victory that has overcome the world—our faith"* (1 John 5:4). God has created us to be *"the head and not the tail...above only, and not...beneath..."* (Deut. 28:13). We must understand that we are fighting *from* a place of victory, not just *for* victory. The power of God resides within *us*; now it is time to release this power.

Our ability to release this power is very much connected to our revelation of who we are. When we have a clear revelation of who God is, we will truly know who we are. We are made in the likeness and in the image of God (see 1 John 3:2). The whole of creation is waiting for the manifestation of the sons and daughters of God. All of creation groans, waiting for our transformation (see Rom. 8:19). Why? We can be divinely confident of this—every demon and all dark forces shall bow when the sons of God appear. This emerging Kingdom Company of overcomers will strike terror into the hearts of God's enemies—just as it was in the days of Jesus (see Mark 1:24). The absolute dominion that God gave Adam was once lost, but it shall now be fully restored as the sons of God walk in authority and power, ruling heavenly places and the earth from a foundation of true love.

Let's start believing what God has declared over our lives. When faith grows exceedingly in our hearts (see 2 Thess. 1:3), we will have this strong inner knowing and conviction: *God has planned for me to be utterly invincible to satan's attack. God has by no means planned any defeat for me. I am unconquerable, clothed in His righteousness and covered by His love. The same immeasurable, unlimited power of Almighty God that raised Christ from the dead is at work within me to overcome every evil* (see 1 John 3:8; 4:4; Eph. 1:19; 3:20).

We are the Lord's Kingdom Company of people, called and commissioned to function as kings and priests.

*And from Jesus Christ, the faithful witness, the firstborn from the dead, and the ruler over the kings of the earth. To Him who loved us and washed us from our sins in His own blood, and has made us kings and priests to His God and Father, to Him be glory and dominion forever and ever. Amen* (Rev. 1:5-6).

This is not some unfounded assertion; Christ Jesus, the *faithful* witness, made this promise to us. He is the One who has washed us from our sins in His own precious, powerful blood.

Without question, the Spirit of God is releasing to this Kingdom Company His Kingdom concepts, which reveal the pathway to overwhelming victory. As Isaiah declared, God's prophets are crying out to prepare the way of the King:

*The voice of one crying in the wilderness: "Prepare the way of the LORD; make straight in the desert a highway for our God. Every valley shall be exalted and every mountain and hill brought low; The crooked places shall be made straight And the rough places smooth; the glory of the LORD shall be revealed, And all flesh shall see it together; for the mouth of the LORD has spoken"* (Isa. 40:3-5).

For the past several decades, the Lord has been releasing prophetic voices across the nation to prepare the way of the Lord. Truly, a highway is being prepared in the desert. The valleys or low places are being filled in. Also, the high places have been pulled down, the crooked places are being made straight, and the stumbling stones are being removed. These promises should cause our souls to rejoice—for the glory of the Lord shall be revealed!

## CHRIST OUR KING

In this season, the Spirit of Truth is highlighting Christ as our King. Much will be released concerning the lordship of Christ (see Col. 1:13-19). With this in mind, our uppermost goal is to advance the King in His Kingdom. Our prayer is for the Kingdom of God to be revealed on earth just as it is in Heaven. Without question, Christ is King of kings and Lord of lords. His directions for us are clear in First Timothy 6:11-16:

> *But you, O man of God, flee these things and pursue righteousness, godliness, faith, love, patience, gentleness. Fight the good fight of faith, lay hold on eternal life, to which you were also called and have confessed the good confession in the presence of many witnesses. I urge you in the sight of God who gives life to all things, and before Christ Jesus who witnessed the good confession before Pontius Pilate, that you keep this commandment without spot, blameless until our Lord Jesus Christ's appearing, which He will manifest in His own time, He who is the blessed and only Potentate, the King of kings and Lord of lords, who alone has immortality, dwelling in unapproachable light, whom no man has seen or can see, to whom be honor and everlasting power. Amen.*

Likewise, Paul prayed that we would *"walk worthy of the Lord...being fruitful...and increasing in the knowledge of God"* (Col. 1:10). Our prayer each day must be *"...on earth as it is in heaven"* (Matt. 6:10) because we need a swift synchronization between our walk and Heaven's will. Just as Christ could say, *"...the Son can do nothing of Himself, but what He sees the Father do"* (John 5:19), we must have a clear focus on our heavenly Father's will as well. When we do this, God will release to us great revelatory light regarding our dominion, and we will understand that we have been granted Kingdom authority to bind and loose (see Matt. 18:18).

It is imperative that we maintain a deep walk in the Word of God (see Ps. 119:9-11). This will bring about the freedom we need to draw near to the Lord. We must approach His holy hill with hearts and hands that are pure (see Ps. 24:4-6). Not only can we *approach* the hill of the Lord, but we can and should *abide* on the hill of the Lord (see Ps. 15:1-2). Each day we must seek to draw ever nearer to Christ, seeking to yield, ever deeper, our will to His will. As we face Him in faith—open and trusting—we will be changed into His likeness (see 2 Cor. 3:18).

## BUSINESS LEADERS

Traditionally, when we have talked about radical followers of Christ—such as this Kingdom Company—we have had this idea that they are primarily in full-time ministry. However, recently the Lord told me that some of the most powerful pastors in the nation are business leaders.

Another aspect of the Kingdom Company will be revealed in the business world. God's Spirit is currently in the process of visiting and radically impacting the business sector. Business leaders are turning to Christ in unprecedented fashion, and the Lord's favor is evident upon these men and women. Moving in God's great grace anointing that is deposited upon their lives, they will help establish God's Kingdom. The Spirit of Truth will release outstanding wisdom, and the result of that wisdom will be increased wealth. This wealth will be released, not for worldly gain, but for God's glory to be revealed around the world.

Expect to see great grace and overflowing favor bestowed upon Christian companies. Remember, it is God who gives us power to get wealth in order to establish His covenants (see Deut. 8:18). We can also expect to see a transfer of wealth— as God promises, *"the wealth of the sinner is stored up for the righteous"* (Prov. 13:22). God will prove Himself faithful to His people, and we can expect the favor of the Lord to rest upon the faithful.

## A SEASON OF SIFTING AND SHIFTING

This has been a season of shaking and transformation. The Spirit of God has been positioning people in order to promote them into their proper place of service. It is vital to be in the right position for the right purpose. In Acts 2:1-5, the followers of Christ were all *"in one place"* and received the promised power. They were in that place because of the prophetic promise of Luke 24:49— *"...tarry in the city of Jerusalem until you are endued with power from on high."*

In many cases, people have been moved from one part of the world to another; this repositioning was necessary to get them into the place of their fruitfulness. For some, this has been a prolonged season of shifts and changes, but it is now coming to an end. Some have been somewhat disorientated; however, those days have come to an end. They will now hear these words, *"This is the way, walk in it"* (Isa. 30:21). They will become like trees that bear fruit, *planted* by the rivers of water (see Ps. 1:3).

We must never forget that God has not just begun our preparation. He has been preparing us for these days all of our lives. We are truly in the Kingdom for such a time as this, and now it is time for promotion. God is moving from strategy to implementation. One of the meanings of the word *promotion* is: "advancement to a more senior job or a higher rank or position." These days of shifting and positioning have helped bring about these advancements. With these spiritual promotions will come a noticeable increase in power—releasing Kingdom power and activating authority.

It is as we *sup* (dine) with Christ Jesus that we are granted to *sit* with Him upon His throne (see Rev. 3:20-22). First comes the supping—true fellowship with Christ; *then* comes the authority and display of Kingdom power. The word *authority* carries with it the implication of "the ability, skill, or capacity to do something." The Kingdom of God is about action, not just mere terminology (see 1 Cor. 4:20). Thus, we can be confident that this promotion from the Lord will give evidence and substance to the reality of a living union with Christ (see Heb. 11:1).

# CHAPTER 4
## *Contend Without Compromise*

While I was waiting on the Lord, seeking to hear what was on His heart, He spoke an extremely strong word. In the most compelling and commanding tone, He said, *"Contend! It is time to take a strong, unshakable stand!"*

This was not a suggestion, but a bold, strong, and stirring *command*, given with such force that it shook me deeply. In the same tone, He also said, *"Sound the alarm! Awaken the warriors!"*

Beloved, we are being called to *contend for change that transforms our culture.* The Holy Spirit spoke to me concerning the *paralyzing passivity* so prevalent in the Church today. As prophetic voices, we must sound the alarm. These are not days of peace! We have no armistice with the workers of darkness! We must *stir ourselves* out of this stupor, as Scripture instructs us to do. We must *rouse to reality and awake* (see Rom. 13:11-14 AMP).

A non-confrontational attitude is not the role and the responsibility of God's end-time warriors! Rather, we must awaken. *Now is the time* to shake ourselves and rise to the occasion (see Josh. 1:7). *We are called to be history-makers, to change the world.* These are not empty phrases, but powerful prophetic promises. Our destinies and the destinies of coming generations demand that we do our very best—*now!* Indeed, the destinies of nations depend upon our actions.

## FLEE COMPROMISE AND COMPLACENCY

This is no time to enter into negotiations with the devil. The enemy of our souls would—*if he could*—utterly destroy and devastate our lives and the lives of our loved ones, our neighbors, and our nations. We must not entertain compromise nor tolerate complacency. On the contrary, we are called to confront the powers of darkness. Rather than remaining passive, complacent, or compromised, we are responsible to resist the enemy and stand firm (see John 10:10). He is a defeated foe—but we, nevertheless, must rout him out of our lives and nations.

Let us fight and withstand, refusing to cooperate in any way with the enemy! Our response must be *the opposite* of his evil suggestions. We must withstand him and his demons with all our hearts, submitting to the Spirit of God and His Word instead. Having done all to stand, we *shall stand* bold and brave, resisting the devil and all his schemes, knowing full well that God's power within us is greater than the devil's power about us (see 1 John 4:4).

## MORE THAN CONQUERORS

When we understand that we are more than conquerors, we will realize that we are fighting from a place of victory! This is true because our Lord and Savior, Christ Jesus, has already defeated every foe at Calvary. In Christ, we are more than conquerors. We are truly, practically, and eternally victorious in every arena of life—and we are *not* victims (see Rom. 8:37). Believe this, beloved. We must cast off any victim mindset and take hold of the truth spoken by Christ as He gave His life for us: *"It is finished"* (John 19:30). He fought the war *and won*—on our behalf.

We will stand strong, knowing that as we resist, we are *more than* victors in Christ Jesus (see Rom. 8:37). What we see withstanding us will not erase from our souls the victory God has promised. May our hearts gain courage from this promise in Deuteronomy 31:6: *"Be strong and of good courage, do not fear nor be afraid of them for the Lord our God, He is the One who goes with you. He will not leave you nor forsake you."* As we stand in faith, drawing ever closer to God and resisting the devil, the enemy will flee (see James 4:7). Through the power of Christ Jesus, we will trample on the evil works of satan (see Luke 10:19). As we walk in confidence, knowing our God and depending upon Christ the King, we will see the promise of Romans 16:20 fulfilled: *the God of Peace will crush the powers of satan under our feet.*

## HOW TO CONTEND

We are at war with the forces of hell; however, we are not fighting alone. The host of Heaven aids us. We must exhort the saints to take a *strong stand* to contend for the true faith. The Book of Jude provides good guidelines for this contending. Though it is long, I am quoting the entire book here because it is so significant to our understanding of this concept.

> *JUDE, A servant of Jesus Christ (the Messiah), and brother of James, [writes this letter] to those who are called (chosen), dearly loved by God the Father and separated (set apart) and kept for Jesus Christ:*
>
> *May mercy, [soul] peace, and love be multiplied to you.*

*Beloved, my whole concern was to write to you in regard to our common salvation. [But] I found it necessary and was impelled to write you and urgently appeal to and exhort [you] to contend for the faith which was once for all handed down to the saints [the faith which is that sum of Christian belief which was delivered verbally to the holy people of God].*

*For certain men have crept in stealthily [gaining entrance secretly by a side door]. Their doom was predicted long ago, ungodly (impious, profane) persons who pervert the grace (the spiritual blessing and favor) of our God into lawlessness and wantonness and immorality, and disown and deny our sole Master and Lord, Jesus Christ (the Messiah, the Anointed One).*

*Now I want to remind you, though you were fully informed once for all, that though the Lord [at one time] delivered a people out of the land of Egypt, He subsequently destroyed those [of them] who did not believe [who refused to adhere to, trust in, and rely upon Him].*

*And angels who did not keep (care for, guard, and hold to) their own first place of power but abandoned their proper dwelling place—these He has reserved in custody in eternal chains (bonds) under the thick gloom of utter darkness until the judgment and doom of the great day.*

*The wicked are sentenced to suffer] just as Sodom and Gomorrah and the adjacent towns—which likewise gave themselves over to impurity and indulged in unnatural vice and sensual perversity—are laid out [in plain sight] as an exhibit of perpetual punishment [to warn] of everlasting fire.*

*Nevertheless in like manner, these dreamers also corrupt the body, scorn and reject authority and government, and revile and libel and scoff at [heavenly] glories (the glorious ones).*

*But when [even] the archangel Michael, contending with the devil, judicially argued (disputed) about the body of Moses, he dared not [presume to] bring an abusive condemnation against him, but [simply] said, The Lord rebuke you!*

*But these men revile (scoff and sneer at) anything they do not happen to be acquainted with and do not understand; and whatever they do understand physically [that which they know by mere instinct], like irrational beasts—by these they corrupt themselves and are destroyed (perish).*

*Woe to them! For they have run riotously in the way of Cain, and have abandoned themselves for the sake of gain [it offers them, following] the error of Balaam, and have perished in rebellion [like that] of Korah!*

*These are hidden reefs (elements of danger) in your love feasts, where they boldly feast sumptuously [carousing together in your midst], without scruples providing for themselves [alone]. They are clouds without water, swept along by the winds; trees, without fruit at the late autumn gathering time—twice (doubly) dead, [lifeless and] plucked up by the roots;*

*Wild waves of the sea, flinging up the foam of their own shame and disgrace; wandering stars, for whom the gloom of eternal darkness has been reserved forever.*

*It was of these people, moreover, that Enoch in the seventh [generation] from Adam prophesied when he said, Behold, the Lord comes with His myriads of holy ones (ten thousands of His saints)*

*To execute judgment upon all and to convict all the impious (unholy ones) of all their ungodly deeds which they have committed [in such an] ungodly [way], and of all the severe (abusive, jarring) things which ungodly sinners have spoken against Him.*

*These are inveterate murmurers (grumblers) who complain [of their lot in life], going after their own desires [controlled by their passions]; their talk is boastful and arrogant, [and they claim to] admire men's persons and pay people flattering compliments to gain advantage.*

*But you must remember, beloved, the predictions which were made by the apostles (the special messengers) of our Lord Jesus Christ (the Messiah, the Anointed One).*

*They told you beforehand, In the last days (in the end time) there will be scoffers [who seek to gratify their own unholy desires], following after their own ungodly passions.*

*It is these who are [agitators] setting up distinctions and causing divisions—merely sensual [creatures, carnal, worldly-minded people], devoid of the [Holy] Spirit and destitute of any higher spiritual life.*

*But you, beloved, build yourselves up [founded] on your most holy faith [make progress, rise like an edifice higher and higher], praying in the Holy Spirit;*

*Guard and keep yourselves in the love of God; expect and patiently wait for the mercy of our Lord Jesus Christ (the Messiah) — [which will bring you] unto life eternal. And refute [so as to] convict some who dispute with you, and on some have mercy who waver and doubt. [Strive to] save others, snatching [them] out of [the] fire; on others take pity [but] with fear, loathing even the garment spotted by the flesh and polluted by their sensuality.*

*Now to Him Who is able to keep you without stumbling or slipping or falling, and to present [you] unblemished (blameless and faultless) before the presence of His glory in triumphant joy and exultation [with unspeakable, ecstatic delight] —*

*To the one only God, our Savior through Jesus Christ our Lord, be glory (splendor), majesty, might and dominion, and power and authority, before all time and now and forever (unto all the ages of eternity). Amen (so be it)* (AMP).

Jude's encouragement to stand strong for truth has never been more necessary than it is today. False teaching and false teachers are multiplying at an alarming rate, and we must expose their lies about loose, unrighteous living and seek the Lord for an outpouring of the Spirit of holiness and the fear of the Lord!

## PUT ON THE ARMOR FOR WAR

Ephesians 6:11-18 offers great advice concerning the best strategy for preparing for this conflict with the powers of darkness. In the very first verse, it says that we must *actively* put on the entire armor provided for us by God:

*Put on God's whole armor [the armor of a heavy-armed soldier which God supplies], that you may be able successfully to stand up against [all] the strategies and the deceits of the devil.*

*For we are not wrestling with flesh and blood [contending only with physical opponents], but against the despotisms, against the powers, against [the master spirits who are] the world rulers of this present darkness, against the spirit forces of wickedness in the heavenly (supernatural) sphere. Therefore put on God's complete armor, that you may be able to resist and stand your ground on the evil day [of danger], and, having done all [the crisis demands], to stand [firmly in your place].*

*Stand therefore [hold your ground], having tightened the belt of truth around your loins and having put on the breastplate of integrity and of moral rectitude and right standing with God,*

*And having shod your feet in preparation [to face the enemy with the firm-footed stability, the promptness, and the readiness produced by the good news] of the Gospel of peace.*

*Lift up over all the [covering] shield of saving faith, upon which you can quench all the flaming missiles of the wicked [one]. And take the helmet of salvation and the sword that the Spirit wields, which is the Word of God. Pray at all times (on every occasion, in every season) in the Spirit, with all [manner of] prayer and entreaty. To that end keep alert and watch with strong purpose and perseverance, interceding in behalf of all the saints (God's consecrated people)* (AMP).

We must be bold, be brave, and be very courageous because we are called to be overcomers, to be aggressive in our stand against the kingdoms of darkness (see Josh. 1:9). Truly, God has given us bold authority to bind the works of satan (see Matt. 16:18-19). And Christ Jesus said that we must take a bold stand against the works of darkness if we are going to see the Kingdom of God advance. In Matthew 11:12, He said,

> *And from the days of John the Baptist until the present time, the kingdom of heaven has endured violent assault, and violent men seize it by force as a precious prize—a share in the heavenly kingdom is sought with most ardent zeal and intense exertion* (AMP).

## TAKE A STAND—NOW

I repeat: *This is a time of confrontation and conflict.* Let us resolve in our hearts that we will neither compromise nor retreat. Instead, let's lift our heads high and resolve that *we, personally*—as those who are empowered by the Holy Spirit and are more than conquerors—are going to make a difference in our generation. Now is the time for us to give our *very best* for the establishing of the Kingdom of God. Now is the time to hold nothing back! Let's make *this hour* our finest hour—to "win for the Lamb the reward of His suffering."

# CHAPTER 5
## *Living Victoriously*

The Spirit of God is encouraging each of us to *advance*, to walk with *clean hands* and a *pure heart*, to draw ever closer to our Lord in this season of *no compromise*, to *move in power*, and to take *the Kingdom for the King!* In many places on the earth, God's people are stirred to pursue true purity; there is a longing in their hearts to not allow anything in their lives that would hinder their walk with Christ Jesus. Second Corinthians 7:1 is a very important verse for this period of time: *"...Beloved, let us cleanse ourselves from all filthiness of the flesh and spirit, perfecting holiness in the fear of God."*

### ADVANCE!

The cry of *"No hesitation!"* has gone forth from Heaven. We are to arise, walk in dominion power, and lay hold of the promises of God. This is not a time to be weak and wavering, but rather a time to be extremely bold and brave. We are commanded to be confident, brave, strong, and very courageous (see Josh. 1:7). The Spirit of God is calling forth the "dread champions." We need to listen with our whole hearts and take courage! God has promised victory! We are called to be the head and not the tail (see Deut. 28:13), and the Holy Spirit who lives within us is greater than the spirit that is at work in the world (see 1 John 4:4). We are created for victory; now is the time to shake ourselves up and declare the proclamation found in Micah 3:8: *"Truly I am full of power by the Spirit of the LORD..."*

We are in the end-time harvest—when the seeds of both good and evil are coming to full fruition. In this time, God is calling for us to arise and take a strong stand against the works of darkness. We are to take the land, as Jesus said: *"The kingdom of heaven suffers violence and violent take it by force"* (Matt. 11:12). This victory will be accomplished by individuals as well as by the corporate Church because the end-time Church will be a people of God's undeniable power (see 1 Cor. 2:1-5). It is time to witness a true demonstration of the power of God's Spirit. The cry has come up before the Lord's throne: *"Oh that You would rend the heavens! That You would come down..."* (Isa. 64:1).

## DRAW EVER CLOSER TO THE LORD

Let us join with the plea of Psalm 90:16-17 and pray:

*Let Your work appear to Your servants, and Your glory to their children. And let the beauty of the LORD our God be upon us, and establish the work of our hands for us...*

The Church should be hungry and desperate to see the works of the Lord. I am weary of seeing the plans and purposes of people; I long to see the mighty acts of God. The Spirit of Truth is calling for us to come into the presence of the Lord. None of us have an excuse. The way is clear, and any one of us can advance higher. The invitation has been extended to all: *"Come up here..."* (Rev. 4:1). When we answer the call to enter the door standing open in Heaven—then we will be able to see more clearly and hear more distinctly. This will, in turn, equip us to advance ever deeper in the anointing on our lives and experience the fulfillment of our divine call.

## DISCOVER DIVINE WISDOM

While ministering recently, I saw what appeared to be a very thin membrane in front of me. I asked, "Lord, what is this?"

The Lord replied, "It is the veil between the earthly realm and the spirit realm—and it is *thinner than ever!*"

We have entered into a season when the Lord Jesus Christ is opening the way to receive *divine light* and *wisdom* like never before. This divine wisdom isn't reserved for the special few, but is available to *all believers* who hunger for intimacy with the Lord and sincerely seek to advance His Kingdom. We will soon discover that God has opened wide a *door of divine revelation* for those who are turning away from the carnal, natural mind and choosing to abide in God's holy presence. Specifically, this divine light and wisdom will lift us up to a higher level in the realm of the Spirit so that the Lord may reveal His *divine strategies* and *powerful plans.* The Lord is extending a very specific invitation to His Bride to "come up here" (see Rev. 4:1) to receive His guidance for His Kingdom's advancement on earth.

## DIVINE WISDOM IS THE PRINCIPAL THING

Beloved, seeking divine wisdom is not an option. Indeed, as believers, we are *commanded* to attain godly wisdom and to prize it as a top priority. Scripture instructs us to obtain wisdom *at all cost.* Consider the admonitions of Proverbs 4:5-9:

> *Get skillful and godly Wisdom, get understanding (discernment, comprehension, and interpretation);*

*do not forget and do not turn back from the words of my mouth.*

*Forsake not [Wisdom], and she will keep, defend, and protect you; love her, and she will guard you.*

*The beginning of Wisdom is: get Wisdom (skillful and godly Wisdom)! [For skillful and godly Wisdom is the principal thing.] And with all you have gotten, get understanding (discernment, comprehension, and interpretation).*

*Prize Wisdom highly and exalt her, and she will exalt and promote you; she will bring you to honor when you embrace her. She shall give to your head a wreath of gracefulness; a crown of beauty and glory will she deliver to you* (AMP).

Elsewhere, it says that we are to seek wisdom above all earthly treasures: *"How much better it is to get skillful and godly Wisdom than gold! And to get understanding is to be chosen rather than silver"* (Prov. 16:16).

## DIVINE WISDOM VERSUS NATURAL UNDERSTANDING

Great advice is released in Proverbs 23:4: *"...Cease from your own [human] wisdom"* (AMP). Mere human, natural knowledge and understanding—*without divine wisdom*—are worthless. Despite our best efforts and intentions, our *natural* minds and human intelligence, without the guidance and illumination of the Holy Spirit, do not have the ability to understand the Word of God, commune with God the Father, or follow the leading of the magnificent person of the Holy Spirit of God. The apostle Paul wrote about this in First Corinthians:

*Eye has not seen, nor ear heard, nor have entered into the heart of man the things which God has prepared for those who love Him. But God has revealed them to us through His Spirit. For the Spirit searches all things, yes, the deep things of God. For what man knows the things of a man except the spirit of the man which is in him? Even so no one knows the things of God except the Spirit of God. Now we have received, not the spirit of the world, but the Spirit who is from God, that we might know the things that have been freely given to us by God. These things we also speak, not in words which man's wisdom teaches but which the Holy Spirit teaches, comparing spiritual things with spiritual. But the natural man does not receive the things of the Spirit of God, for they are foolishness to him; nor can he know them, because they are spiritually discerned. But he who is spiritual judges all things, yet he himself is rightly judged by no one. For "who has known the mind of the Lord that he may instruct Him?" But we have the mind of Christ* (1 Cor. 2:1-16).

Our *natural* minds are not merely insufficient, but following our carnal thoughts and reasoning is actually *enmity* toward God. This is a serious matter, beloved. In Romans, Paul wrote:

*For to be carnally minded is death; but to be spiritually minded is life and peace. Because the carnal mind is enmity against God: for it is not subject to the law of God, neither indeed can be* (Rom. 8:6-7).

As disciples of Christ, we dare not continue to rely on our natural minds, but we must renew our minds to become "spiritually minded." If we don't renew our minds, our *lack of knowledge* of the Holy One will eventually lead to our destruction. The Spirit of God warns us with an exceptionally blunt truth on this matter in Hosea 4:6: *"My people are destroyed for lack of knowledge...*" This Scripture is not speaking about mere human knowledge, but about divine enlightenment—*wisdom from above.* We face destruction if we fail to appropriate divine wisdom—if we continue to live according to our own human reasoning.

This is not the season to stumble about in the maze of human philosophy or psychology, vainly speculating about the future or resurrecting past offenses that have already been forgiven. These mental speculations and examinations may seem righteous and even holy, but Scripture warns us that there is a way that *appears* right unto people, but is actually the way of death and destruction (see Prov. 14:12).

We must allow the Word of God to become "flesh of our flesh" by replacing the carnal pathways of worldly reasoning and beliefs with the person of the Lord Jesus Christ, as revealed to us in Scripture:

> *And be not conformed to this world: but be ye transformed by the renewing of your mind, that ye may prove what is that good, and acceptable, and perfect, will of God* (Rom. 12:2).

## DIVINE WISDOM IN HOLINESS AND THE FEAR OF THE LORD

*No treasure in Heaven or on earth* is more precious than this wisdom from above—wisdom that is actually the *person* of Christ our Lord! This is why divine wisdom is so extremely important and, indeed, priceless. Wisdom, in fact, is Christ Himself. Paul stated this fact so clearly in his first letter to the church at Corinth:

> *...Christ the power of God, and the wisdom of God* (1 Cor. 1:24).

> *But of him are ye in Christ Jesus, who of God is made unto us wisdom...* (1 Cor. 1:30 KJV).

God is offering to each of us a much higher wisdom, which is released by the Spirit of God. Now is the time to embrace true wisdom, who is Christ Himself.

Many are asking, *"How do we obtain this much-desired Divine Wisdom?"* It is the passionate quest and resounding question throughout human history. The Holy Scriptures clearly reveal the answer:

> *But to man He said, Behold, the reverential and worshipful fear of the Lord—that is Wisdom; and to depart from evil is understanding* (Job 28:28 AMP).

> *The reverent fear and worship of the Lord is the beginning of Wisdom and skill [the preceding and the first essential, the prerequisite and the alphabet]; a good understanding, wisdom, and meaning have all those who do [the will of the Lord]. Their praise of Him endures forever* (Ps. 111:10 AMP).

> *The reverent and worshipful fear of the Lord is the beginning and the principal and choice part of knowledge [its starting point and its essence]; but fools despise skillful and godly Wisdom, instruction, and discipline* (Prov. 1:7 AMP).

> *The reverent and worshipful fear of the Lord is the beginning (the chief and choice part) of Wisdom, and the knowledge of the Holy One is insight and understanding* (Prov. 9:10 AMP).

What are the first steps to receiving the wisdom from above? This way of the Lord's divine wisdom is entered through two gates—*holiness* (as expressed in humility) and *reverence* or *fear of the Lord*. These are the gates leading to the pathway of wisdom. As the Bible says, God resists the proud, but He gives grace to the humble (see Prov. 3:34; 1 Pet. 5:5). Humility is really important. The grace that He bestows upon the humble is the *divine ability* to know Him and His strategies for bringing His Kingdom to earth—the grace for divine wisdom.

## DIVINE WISDOM THROUGH THE HOLY SPIRIT

The Holy Spirit alone imparts divine wisdom, as Christ explained in John 16:13:

*But when He, the Spirit of Truth (the Truth-giving Spirit) comes, He will guide you into all the Truth (the whole, full Truth). For He will not speak His own message [on His own authority]; but He will tell whatever He hears [from the Father; He will give the message that has been given to Him], and He will announce and declare to you the things that are to come [that will happen in the future]* (AMP).

The teacher who will lead us into wisdom is God's Holy Spirit. The Spirit alone—not our natural minds—can guide us into all truth, who is Christ Jesus. Specifically, the Spirit *"will announce and declare to you the things that are to come [that will happen in the future]."*

This truth is so vital for today! As world economies implode, retirement savings dwindle, and earthquakes, tsunamis, famines, and floods devastate communities, it would seem that the entire world is seeking to know *what will happen in the future.* Without a real relationship with Christ Jesus, humanity cannot find true wisdom. These are days of strong and deep deception, and most of humanity is deluded, blind to the truth, and stumbling toward death and destruction (see Matt. 7:13). As men and women continue to reject Christ, spirits of fear, accusation, bitterness, anger, occultism, envy, jealousy, and rejection divide and destroy families, neighborhoods, and nations.

These days that we are facing demand that all believers move and speak in *revelatory*—not natural—understanding of the times and seasons, receiving godly guidance as we embrace the promise of Nehemiah 9:20, which assures us that God will release to us the Spirit of God to guide us. As true followers of Christ, we walk as light-bearers in a dark age. Through us, the Spirit of God will release divine wisdom to set men and women free from the captivity of satan's lies (see John 8:12). In these days, God's children will finally shine with divine wisdom, Christ Himself. To do this, we must rely *only* on the revelatory light and illumination of Christ and share His wisdom with those whose minds are shrouded by lies and deceptions.

## DIVINE WISDOM THROUGH THE WORD OF GOD

A good, practical exercise for gaining divine wisdom is to study a chapter in the Book of Proverbs each and every day. Many will be surprised at the sound wisdom that will be imparted to them by the Spirit of God. The greatest textbook on life is the Holy Bible; within its pages are the insights that will transform our entire outlook on life (see Ps. 119:9-11). Because of that reality, we must take time each day to feed our souls with Heaven's manna.

As we do, we approach the Lord with reverence and awe, humbling ourselves before His majesty. We come not with our own holiness and righteousness, but clothed in Christ! We can approach His throne of grace boldly and ask our Father God with a sincere heart for the wisdom of Christ. Let us ask the Holy Spirit to enlighten the eyes of our understanding, which is exactly what Paul prayed for us as well:

*That the God of our Lord Jesus Christ, the Father of glory, may give unto you the spirit of wisdom and revelation in the knowledge of him: The eyes of your understanding being enlightened... (Eph. 1:17-18).*

If we ask in simple faith, believing His Word, God will liberally bestow this much-needed wisdom in our hearts:

*If any of you is deficient in wisdom, let him ask of the giving God [Who gives] to everyone liberally and ungrudgingly, without reproaching or faultfinding, and it will be given him* (James 1:5 AMP).

The benefits and blessings of divine wisdom are enormous. Wisdom produces understanding, which brings prosperity and favor. As Proverbs says, *"He who keeps understanding shall prosper and find good"* (Prov. 19:8). Further, Christ Jesus states that as we seek first His Kingdom, everything else will be put into proper place (see Matt. 6:33).

## DIVINE WISDOM TO PREACH CHRIST IN POWER

As we humble ourselves and seek God *"with clean hands and a pure heart"* (Ps. 24:4), the Spirit of Council will release to us the much needed divine wisdom for our day. God desires to release revelation and discernment on a higher level, bringing us out of the world's confusion and chaos. As we renew our minds with the Word of God, we will *know* God, and we will shine ever brighter and do great exploits (see Dan. 11:32).

Those great exploits include preaching Christ in the power of the Spirit because our witness of the gospel is not to be with *"persuasive words of human wisdom"* (see 1 Cor. 1:17), but, as Paul continues, *"...in demonstration of the Spirit and of power, that your faith should not be in the wisdom of men but in the power of God"* (1 Cor. 2:4-5). In order to experience the *power* of God, Paul knew that he required the *divine wisdom* of God—not mere human reasoning. Paul wrote that he did not speak *"the wisdom of this age, nor of the rulers of this age,"* but rather he spoke *"the wisdom of*

*God in a mystery, the hidden wisdom which God ordained before the ages for our glory"* (1 Cor. 2:6-7).

Beloved, let's all contend for the prize possession of Christ—the wisdom of God! Earnestly, we must desire this divine wisdom, seeking Him above all else, and prepare to witness the mighty power of the Lord to love the addicted and lost, minister to the poor, heal the sick, raise the dead, prophesy to nations, and advance the Kingdom of God on earth—through our own hands and hearts!

# CHAPTER 6
## *Qualified and Commissioned*

Many believers feel unqualified for the work God has called them to do; however, that is contrary to what the Bible actually says:

> *Such is the reliance and confidence that we have through Christ toward and with reference to God. Not that we are fit (qualified and sufficient in ability) of ourselves to form personal judgments or to claim or count anything as coming from us; but our power and ability and sufficiency are from God. [It is He] Who has qualified us (making us to be fit and worthy and sufficient) as ministers and dispensers of a new covenant [of salvation through Christ], not [ministers] of the letter— that is of legally written code—but of the Spirit; for the code [of the law] kills, but the [Holy] Spirit makes alive (2 Cor. 3:4-6 AMP).*

What a wonderful and encouraging word! By the power of God, each of us is deemed qualified and able to do the will of God. We know this is not our own ability, but rather because of the grace of God upon our lives. These verses declare that by the grace of God and the anointing of the Spirit, we are fit and worthy and sufficient ministers.

One of satan's most common tools is to lie to us about who we really are! To counter his lies, let's look at what God says about us in Philippians 2:13: *"For it is God which works in you both to will and to do of His good pleasure."* We must remember that God is at work in us in order to work through us. He desires something to be done in our lives, and He will work it out. God never gives us a task without also giving us a touch to accomplish it. Paul encouraged the Philippians with this very truth:

> *I have strength for all things in Christ Who empowers me—I am ready for anything and equal to anything through Him Who infuses inner strength into me, [that is, I am self-sufficient in Christ's sufficiency]* (Phil. 4:13 AMP).

This is a very strong promise! By the grace of God, we are infused with strength, empowered, and equipped for anything the Lord wants us to do. It is time to stop agreeing with the enemy of our souls and to start saying about ourselves what God has said about us. The devil will always attempt to administer weakness to us, but we must learn to talk a good talk in order to walk a good walk. *"...Let the weak say, I am strong [a warrior]!"* (Joel 3:10 AMP). The Word of God encourages us to be strong in the power of God's might, assuring us that if God is for us—and He is most assuredly—no one can be against us (see Rom. 8:31). However, in order to overcome the devil by the blood of Jesus, we must boldly proclaim our testimony. *"And they overcame him by the blood of the Lamb, and by the word of their testimony; and they loved not their lives unto the death"* (Rev. 12:11).

It is time to do a study of the promises and provisions in the Word of God that tell us who we are and what we can expect. Peter reminds us that these *"...exceedingly great and precious promises..."* are given to help us become who we are

(2 Pet. 1:4). When the promises of the Word of God become firmly rooted in our hearts, we will be able to boldly declare, *"...truly I am full of power by the Spirit of the LORD..."* (Mic. 3:8).

David was a great warrior, and one of his strengths was that he constantly reminded himself of what God was doing in him. When he was facing one of his most difficult circumstances, the Bible tells us that *"...David strengthened himself in the LORD his God"* (1 Sam. 30:6). David also meditated on what God had done through him: *"For You girded me with strength for the battle; those who rose up against me You subdued under me"* (2 Sam. 22:40 AMP). This is a great example for us to follow. We need to have a grasp on the mighty things the Lord has done in us and through us!

## DECLARING THE TRUTH OF WHO WE ARE

The enemy will see us as we see ourselves. Thus, we will never take the land the Lord has for us unless we get rid of our "grasshopper complex." This is what happened to the ten spies, who said: *"There we saw the giants (the descendants of Anak came from the giants); and we were like grasshoppers in our own sight, and so we were in their sight"* (Num. 13:33). We must not let this happen. Rather, this is a time to fill our hearts with the Word of God. If we walk in the Word, we will walk in the true light. As the psalms say, *"Your word is a lamp for my feet and a light on my path"* (Ps. 119:105 NIV), and *"The unfolding of your words gives light; it gives understanding to the simple"* (Ps. 119:130 NIV).

Our faith will be built up if we fill our souls with the Word of God, for *"...faith comes by hearing, and hearing by the word of God"* (Rom. 10:17). Like Jeremiah, we must eat the Word of God so that it becomes the rejoicing of our hearts:

*"Your words were found, and I ate them, and Your word was to me the joy and rejoicing of my heart, for I am called by your name, O LORD God of hosts"* (Jer. 15:16). Truly, the Word of God is perfect. Notice the amazing benefits of walking in the Word listed in this psalm:

*The law of the LORD is perfect, converting the soul; the testimony of the LORD is sure, making wise the simple; the statutes of the LORD are right, rejoicing the heart; The commandment of the LORD is pure, enlightening the eyes; the fear of the LORD is clean, enduring forever; the judgments of the LORD are true and righteous altogether. More to be desired are they than gold, Yea, than much fine gold; sweeter also than honey and the honeycomb. Moreover by them Your servant is warned, and in keeping them there is great reward* (Ps. 19:7-11).

## LIFE'S QUESTIONS

I firmly believe that all true questions are fully answered in the Word of God. A very important question is posed, "How can a young person live a pure and meaningful life?" Let us search out the answer to this question in order to lay hold of eternal truth. The Word of God contains the answers for all of humankind's questions. As these treasures of truth are revealed, they will not only aid young people, but people of all ages, in all walks of life, and of all races—regardless of their background. This is a very important question because each and every one of us should desire to accomplish all that is possible in our lifetimes. Each of us should desire to truly live lives worth living. The promise of the Word of God is, *"...you shall know the truth, and the truth shall make you free"* (John 8:32). Now is the time to go on a quest for truth:

*How can a young man cleanse his way? By taking*

*heed according to Your word. With my whole heart
I have sought You; oh, let me not wander from Your
commandments! Your word I have hidden in my heart,
that I might not sin against You. Blessed are You, O
LORD! Teach me Your statutes* (Ps. 119:9-12).

One of the first things we need to address is the issue of humanity's need for correction and cleansing. We must first realize that people are born in sin. In the Word of God, we discover our true condition, but also we rejoice to see the answer to humanity's problem was provided by the complete sacrifice of Christ Jesus. In the Word of God, we find that all have sinned and come short of the glory of God (see Rom. 3:23). Also Romans 6:23 says that the wages of sin is death, which speaks of eternal separation from God. We are truly lost, undone, and in need of salvation.

In the Bible, we also find the loving heart of God revealed; His love for humankind is so great that He was willing to give His only Son to pay the debt for humankind's sins (see John 3:16). What an awesome God! The doorway of salvation is open wide to all who will come to Christ. All those who come to Christ in simple faith, God will receive. The choice rests with people. If they open their hearts to Christ by faith, repent of their sins, and turn to Jesus for full and free salvation, they will then be transformed into new creatures, passing from spiritual death to spiritual life (see Rom. 10:9-13; 2 Cor. 5:17).

As followers of Christ, we are instructed to hide the Word of God in our hearts. This means that we are to memorize the Scriptures—not just committing the words and phrases to memory, but rather having them as living directives for our lives. Truly, the Word of God never grows old. It is like looking at a beautiful diamond, which we never see in the same way twice. The more light that is shining upon the diamond, the more brilliance it reflects. So it is with the Bible; the more revelatory light that people have—the deeper and richer the Scriptures become to them. We are instructed to pray, asking God to open our eyes so that we can behold wonderful insights from His Word. I have had many people say to me, "I just cannot understand the Scriptures." We need to come to the realization that the Holy Spirit is the author of the Bible.

> *All scripture is given by inspiration of God, and is profitable for doctrine, for reproof, for correction, for instruction in righteousness: that the man of God may be perfect, thoroughly furnished unto all good works* (2 Tim. 3:16-17).

The Scriptures also teach us that the natural mind is not able to understand the things of the Spirit (see 1 Cor. 2:9-14). If we want to understand what God's Word is saying, we must approach the Scriptures—not with our natural minds, but with our hearts. Let's ask the Holy Spirit to be our teacher and our guide; these are part of His ministry to the Body of Christ. As Jesus promised in John 14:26:

> *But the Comforter, which is the Holy Ghost, whom the Father will send in my name, he shall teach you all things, and bring all things to your remembrance, whatsoever I have said unto you* (KJV).

What an awesome promise! The author of the Bible abides inside each believer to be our teacher! That means that each one of us, as Christians, has the teacher—the Holy Spirit—residing and abiding within us. For this reason, we must ask Him to guide our hearts and minds into the deeper truths of the Word of God.

## THE WORD OF GOD IS A LIVING WORD

In Hebrews 4:12, we are informed that,

> *...the word of God is living and powerful, and sharper*

*than any two-edged sword, piercing even to the division of soul and spirit, and of joints and marrow, and is a discerner of the thoughts and intents of the heart.*

While the Scripture does reveal the truth about our lives, it also reveals the truth about our hearts—as the wording of this passage shows: *"the word of God is living"* and active, penetrating and getting to the very deep secrets of our hearts. As we ponder the Word of God, we discover the motives of our hearts. Be very sure, only God knows the true intent of our hearts (see Jer. 17:9-10). Daily each of us should ask God to turn the search light of His Word upon our hearts to reveal any and all hidden agendas. *"Search me, O God, and know my heart: try me, and know my thoughts: and see if there be any wicked way in me, and lead me in the way everlasting"* (Ps. 139:23).

Yes, the Word of God is a true revealer of the depths of people's hearts. As we take time to truly study the Scriptures, we will find the wonderful wisdom of God. The promise is that the Word will be a bright lamp to our pathway (see Ps. 119:105), and if we will walk in this pathway of light, we will receive understanding (see Ps. 119:130). No one needs to stumble around in the darkness of this world when we can and must choose to walk in the light of the Word of God. He alone can give wisdom and understanding to each and every issue of our lives.

## THE WORD OF GOD IS POWERFUL AND PRODUCTIVE

In Isaiah 55:11, we find this prophetic promise concerning God's Word. God declares:

*So shall My word be that goes forth from My mouth; it shall not return to Me void, but it shall accomplish what I please, and it shall prosper in the thing for which I sent it.*

Never forget that when God speaks, unlimited power is released. Nothing can withstand the power of His Word. When God speaks, things are accomplished (see Ps. 29:1-9). We are reminded that the grass will dry up and the flowers will fade, but the Word of God will last forever. So we see that the Word of God is powerful, productive, and permanent. *"But the word of the LORD endures forever. Now this is the word which by the gospel was preached to you"* (1 Pet. 1:25). The Book of Psalms says, *"Forever, O LORD, Your word is settled in heaven"* (Ps. 119:89). The Word of God is ageless; it never grows old nor passes away. In Matthew 5:18, we are told that, as long as Heaven and earth continue, not one line or punctuation mark will be removed from the eternal Word of God. The Word of God is steadfast and sure; it does not change with the whims of people. *"The law of the LORD is perfect, converting the soul: the testimony of the Lord is sure making wise the simple"* (Ps. 19:7).

The Word of God will also bring joy and rejoicing to the hearts of people (see Ps. 19:7-14). In Job 23:12, we find that the study of the Word of God is more important to Job than the desire for "necessary food." Again, in Psalm 119:103, we discover that the Word of God is sweeter to our taste than honey. We are instructed to deeply desire the Word of God. Just as a newborn baby needs milk to grow, we too must have the meat of the Word of God to continue our spiritual growth (see 1 Pet. 2:2).

A more in-depth look into Psalm 19 reveals that we will receive true and necessary enlightenment from the study of the Scriptures. We are able to read of the worth and endless value of the Word of God, which is more desirable than fine gold, and we learn that there is great protection when we walk in the light of the Word of God. In Jeremiah, the Word of God is compared to fire and a hammer. *"'Is not my word like a fire?' says the LORD, 'And like a hammer that breaks the rock in pieces'"* (Jer. 23:29). This passage deals with the power of the Word of God to tear down as well as build up and also to purify. Building and purifying are very important issues on the Father's heart.

## LIKE A FIRE

The Word of God is like fire. This fire will refine what is precious and remove what is worthless from our lives. It is time to embrace the divine fire. God's fire will only make more precious what is of value in our lives, and it will consume that which is worthless according to First Corinthians 3:13-15. We also see the promise of God's prophetic word being likened to fire in Jeremiah 5:14.

## LIKE A HAMMER

A hammer can be used to construct as well as destroy. I believe we are entering into a time when the Word of God will become an active hammer to destroy what people have been busy building with their religious plans and misguided ambitions. Toward the beginning of history, people said, "Let us build a tower into heaven." When God came down and confused their languages, all the effort that the people had given toward constructing their tower was brought to nothing (see Gen. 11:1-9). This will be the case again. The hammer of God will fall upon all that is being built that He has not sanctioned. We must be busy advancing the Kingdom of God, not busy attempting to build our own kingdoms.

## LIKE A WEAPON

The apostle Paul stated that the Word of God is a weapon. In Ephesians 6:17, we are instructed to *"take...the sword of the Spirit, which is the word of God."* The only offensive weapon we have is the sword of the Spirit—the Word of God. Oh how powerful this weapon is! We must take time to fill our souls with the pure Word of God so that when the foe attempts to bring something against us, we can effectively retaliate with God's Word. Our example for using the Word against the devil comes directly from Christ in Matthew 4:1-10. Each time the devil brought a temptation before Christ Jesus, He would speak forth the truth of God's Word. This is our pattern for standing against the wiles of the devil. This is why it is so crucial for us to take time to study and hide the Word in our hearts—so that we will be well-equipped to stand firm against all attacks of the devil.

## THE OVERLOOKED TREASURE

I one time heard a story about a very wealthy woman who had only one wayward grandson to inherit the family's wealth. She knew, however, that he did not live for Christ and that he would soon waste the wealth on wicked living. Many times she had spoken to him about the love of God and the benefits of serving the Lord. Her words were to no avail; he simply continued to live for himself, seeking the empty and fleeting pleasures of this life.

One day after her death, the wicked grandson was called to the family lawyer's office for the reading of his affluent grandmother's will. The lawyer opened the last will and testament of the dear old saint, and it was a letter to her grandson. She said "I am leaving you my most treasured possession—my Bible; in it you will find everything you will ever need."

The lawyer said "Well young man, all you get is what she left for you—her Bible." In a rage, the young man took the old well-worn Bible, threw it into a bag, and carried it home, planning never to open its pages. After years of living a helpless, barren life of poverty, now sick from his sinful lifestyle, he lay dying. In his last moments of life, he thought of his grandmother and how she had faced her time of death with peace. So he found the old family Bible, which he had never opened, until now. As he slowly opened the Bible, to his utter amazement, he discovered a cashier's check made out to him from his grandmother. She had left her entire fortune to him, hidden away in her Bible. He had lived in deep dearth and pitiful poverty, not aware that just inside the Bible was the answer to his money needs. May each of us learn from his sad story; may we never neglect the treasure of the Word of God. Truly, all the answers to our needs are found within the Living Word of God.

Let us keep the Word deep within our hearts, because out of the abundance of the heart the mouth speaks (see Matt. 12:34). If we have hearts filled with doubt and fear, then that is exactly what we will speak forth. Instead, we must let the Word of God dwell in us richly (see Col. 3:16). Solomon confirmed the crucial role played by our hearts when he wrote: *"Keep thy heart with all diligence; for out of it are the issues of life"* (Prov. 4:23 KJV) and, *"For as he thinks in his heart, so is he..."* (Prov. 23:7).

## PRAYING THE WORD

If we will learn to pray back to God what He has promised us in His Word, we will be greatly aided in getting our prayers answered. Notice this promise found in First John 5:14-15:

*And this is the confidence that we have in him, that, if we ask any thing according to his will, he hears us: And if we know that he hear us, whatsoever we ask, we know that we have the petitions that we desired of him* (KJV).

When we decree what God has decreed, we will see some mighty things begin to take place! Many pray and do not get an answer because they are praying outside of the will of God. Some people even go without food, calling it a fast, when God sees it as a mere hunger strike! In this way, some use fasting as an attempt to pressure Him into a reply. Instead, we must be taught to truly pray (see Luke 11:1-2).

Job 22:27-28 speaks of this tremendous power that we have in prayer:

> *You will make your prayer to Him, He will hear you, and you will pay your vows. You will also decree a thing, and it will be established for you; so light will shine on your ways.*

The Word of God also promises that *"whatever things you ask when you pray, believe that you receive them, and you will have them"* (Mark 11:24). Jesus reminded us that God longs to answer our prayers (see John 16:23-24). He also said, *"If ye abide in me, and my words abide in you, ye shall ask what ye will, and it shall be done unto you"* (John 15:7 KJV).

The power of God resides in us! As the apostle John wrote, *"You are of God, little children, and have overcome them, because He who is in you is greater than he who is in the world"* (1 John 4:4). God has promised that, through Him, we can accomplish anything (see Luke 1:37). As the apostle Paul put it, *"Nay, in all these things we are more than conquerors through him that loved us"* (Rom. 8:37 KJV).

Now is the time to ask God for big things. If we ask, we will receive because we know that nothing is too big for our God. The promise of this passage is really true for us:

> *Now to Him who is able to do exceedingly abundantly above all that we ask or think, according to the power*

*that works in us, to Him be glory in the church by Christ Jesus to all generations, forever and ever. Amen* (Eph. 3:20-21).

As we read such verses, we need to ask God to enlarge our vision!

## DO NOT LET FEAR ROB YOU

This is not a time to be fearful, but a time to be very strong and courageous. Remember the command found in the Book of Joshua:

*Be strong and courageous, because you will lead these people to inherit the land I swore to their forefathers to give them. Be strong and very courageous. Be careful to obey all the law my servant Moses gave you; do not turn from it to the right or to the left, that you may be successful wherever you go. Do not let this Book of the Law depart from your mouth; meditate on it day and night, so that you may be careful to do everything written in it. Then you will be prosperous and successful. Have I not commanded you? Be strong and courageous. Do not be terrified; do not be discouraged, for the LORD your God will be with you wherever you go* (Josh. 1:6-9 NIV).

Fear is the foe of faith. We must not let fear rob us. Instead, let's start standing on the promises of the Word of God. When we do, we will find that our spiritual houses are firmly founded on the solid rock of Jesus Christ. We will stand even when the winds of adversity begin to blow. God will give us great grace for these days as we reach out to a hurting world with the message of His love.

The Word of God has a great deal to say about the dangers of fear. Here are two verses that I have found particularly helpful in overcoming the lies of fear:

*Fear thou not; for I am with thee: be not dismayed; for I am thy God: I will strengthen thee; yea, I will help thee; yea, I will uphold thee with the right hand of my righteousness* (Isa. 41:10 KJV).

*For God hath not given us the spirit of fear; but of power, and of love, and of a sound mind* (2 Tim. 1:7 KJV).

## IT'S TIME TO GET TO KNOW GOD

The words recorded by the prophet Hosea remind us of the perilous times we live in, advising us that it is time to seek the Lord until He comes and reigns righteousness upon us (see Hos. 10:12). Elsewhere we are also told that we will only find the Lord when we search for Him with all our hearts (see Jer. 29:12-13). Jesus said that we are to seek first the Kingdom of God, and if we truly seek His Kingdom first, He will take care of all of our needs (see Matt. 6:33).

However, if we seek first to take care of our own kingdoms, the opposite will be true. We could be like the people of Haggai's day, who worked very hard, only to put their money in a bag with holes in it (see Hag. 1:6). This is a real warning as we see the days ahead, when many banks and money markets will be shaken. The only secure place to be is seeking first the Kingdom of God! The Scripture passage below presents a beautiful picture of the Lord's sufficiency and strength for those who spend time in His presence:

*Have you not known? Have you not heard? The everlasting God, the LORD, the Creator of the ends of the earth, neither faints nor is weary. His understanding is unsearchable. He gives power to the weak, and to those who have no might He increases strength. Even the youths shall faint and be weary, and the young men shall utterly fall, but those who*

*wait on the LORD shall renew their strength; they
shall mount up with wings like eagles, they shall run
and not be weary, they shall walk and not faint* (Isa.
40:28-31).

My prayer is that we will get to know Him better and
better. May we be gripped with a desperate hunger for God,
for that is the key to receiving His supernatural unction to
function in these last days. Remember, *"...the people who
know their God will display strength and take action"* (Dan.
11:32 NASB).

# CHAPTER 7
## *Delighting the Lord*

*The LORD bless you and keep you; the LORD make His face shine upon you, and be gracious to you; the LORD lift up His countenance upon you, and give you peace. So they shall put My name on the children of Israel, and I will bless them* (Num. 6:24-27).

God said about His Son Jesus, *"This is My beloved Son in whom I am well pleased"* (Matt. 17:5), and He desires to be able to state the very same thing about us. We too can have this acclaim from the Father if our foremost goal is to bring God "good pleasure!" The Spirit of God is placing great emphasis upon the establishing of God's Kingdom, and the cry has gone forth, *"...on earth as it is in heaven"* (Matt. 6:10). True contentment abounds and joy overflows when we recognize that our lives are delighting the Lord. Nothing in this world can convey such a feeling of achievement as accomplishing what God has given us to do. Our highest purpose and most noble quest should be to live in such a manner as to make everything we do fully pleasing to the Lord (see Col. 1:9-10).

The apostle Paul penned these incredibly encouraging words in Philippians 2:13: *"For it is God who works in you, both to will and to do for His good pleasure."* Notice the promise of co-laboring with God: It is God working within us both to will and to work for His good pleasure. Our question should be, "Just what is it that brings God this good pleasure?" The answer is as follows: We discover (from Christ) that finding a people in whom He can release true Kingdom authority brings God the Father good pleasure. *"It is your Father's good pleasure to give you the kingdom"* (Luke 12:32). There will be a swift advancing of the Kingdom message across the entire Body of Christ during these days. I am so encouraged already by the way I see God's Kingdom emerging.

When God calls and commissions people for a task, He always provides the power to accomplish the deed. Remember, through Christ we can do all things (see Phil. 4:13). Something exhilarating and electrifying happens when the Holy Spirit is in control and we are in the right place for the right reason. Like Esther, we too are in the Kingdom for such a time as this (see Esther 4:14). We can find such a feeling of satisfaction knowing that we are in the right place for the right purpose—knowing that we're doing what God has destined us to do. This is the life that is contented and fruitful. He has destined us to live like this because He has called us to redeem the time, to make the most of each moment (see Eph. 5:15-17).

Let's set our goals higher and never settle for second best because God desires to give us Kingdom power. It is true— we will find Him when we set our whole hearts to seek Him (see Jer. 29:12-13).

## EMPOWERED TO BOLDLY FACE THE FUTURE

We must not let our *past failures* keep us from our *future victories*. Great grace is offered for each of us to get over past failures. It makes no difference how twisted and tangled our lives have been or even are right now; God is able. God always makes a way to free us from our past. We are in a season of refreshing and restoring. This is a new day, and old things have passed away. Now God is releasing divine favor to us so that we can accomplish great exploits for the glory of God. Even the wounds that we have suffered can become great avenues for healing; after all, it was by Christ's stripes that we are healed. When we are healed from our wounds, we will receive grace for healing. God's overflowing mercies are new every morning, and His faithfulness is great. Let's invite God's new day to dawn upon our lives (see Lam. 3:22-23).

We must never give up and never give in. We are warned in Hebrews 10:35 to never give up our confidence and hope because it carries with it great grace and spiritual reward. The bottom line is, we are created for success, and God has confidence in us. Remember, we are each His choice. God is saying to some of us, *"Try again."* Even if we did not succeed in the previous attempts, we must not lose heart—it is time to regroup and try again, knowing that failure is never God's plan. We are going to see doors open that were closed to us previously because God is granting breakthrough. God promises that even if our sins are red like crimson, they can be washed white as snow (see Isa. 1:18). One of the sweetest words in the human language is the word *forgiven!*

## TURN GOD'S PROMISES INTO YOUR PROVISION

The apostle Paul instructed us to walk purposefully toward one true goal—the upward call of God (see Phil. 3:12-16). This is not a time to wander around the mountain of defeat and unbelief; instead, we are to lay hold of the promises of God, take Him at His Word, and stand firm in faith. Recently,

God released to me this very encouraging statement: "This will be the season when My people begin to believe what they know. My Word will move from the head, to the heart, to the hands."

Rather than just being content to sit and hear, we will become activators of the Word. God has destined us to walk in victory, not defeat. We are called to be victors, not victims. We must never forget God's promise that: *"No weapon formed against you shall prosper..."* (Isa. 54:17).

The Body of Christ stands poised at the very verge of *the greatest move of God in the history of humankind.* Each of us should expect swift and radical change. We do not have any more time for another trip around the mountain; we *must* enter into the promises of God today. No matter how confused and confounded we have been in the past, this is the day when we can find the exit sign and end the wilderness wanderings. We can begin to walk in our purpose while seeking first the Kingdom of God.

*Therefore we make it our aim...to be well pleasing to Him* (2 Cor. 5:9).

# CHAPTER 8
## *The Blood of Christ*

The Spirit of Truth, at this point in time, is focusing our attention upon the finished work of Christ and His sacrifice for sin. Prepare to hear much about the precious blood of Christ. As Peter the apostle stated:

> *Knowing that you were not redeemed with corruptible things, like silver or gold, from your aimless conduct received by tradition from your fathers, but with the precious blood of Christ, as of a lamb without blemish and without spot. He indeed was foreordained before the foundation of the world, but was manifest in these last times for you who through Him believe in God, who raised Him from the dead and gave Him glory, so that your faith and hope are in God* (1 Pet. 1:18-21).

The blood of Christ will be preached in great power. Once again, we will sing songs concerning the power and purpose of the victorious blood of the Lamb. Let's allow the words of these precious powerful old hymns wash over our souls until they stir our hearts and cause the question of eternity to sweep our souls. Let's ponder the questions asked in these powerful hymns.

## Are You Washed in the Blood?

*Elisha A. Hoffman (1839-1929)*

Have you been to Jesus for the cleansing power?
Are you washed in the blood of the Lamb?
Are you fully trusting in His grace this hour?
Are you washed in the blood of the Lamb?

*Refrain*
Are you washed in the blood,
In the soul-cleansing blood of the Lamb?
Are your garments spotless? Are they white as snow?
Are you washed in the blood of the Lamb?

Are you walking daily by the Savior's side?
Are you washed in the blood of the Lamb?
Do you rest each moment in the Crucified?
Are you washed in the blood of the Lamb?

When the Bridegroom cometh will your robes be white?
Are you washed in the blood of the Lamb?
Will your soul be ready for His presence bright,
And be washed in the blood of the Lamb?

Lay aside the garments that are stained with sin,
And be washed in the blood of the Lamb;
There's a fountain flowing for the soul unclean,
O be washed in the blood of the Lamb.

Our hearts and souls will be stirred and our passion aroused by the words of this next precious song concerning the blood of Christ:

### There Is a Fountain Filled with Blood
*William Cowper (1731-1800)*

There is a fountain filled with blood drawn from
    Immanuel's veins;
And sinners, plunged beneath that flood, lose all their
    guilty stains:
Lose all their guilty stains, lose all their guilty stains;
And sinners, plunged beneath that flood lose all their
    guilty stains.

The dying thief rejoiced to see that fountain in his day;
And there have I, though vile as he, wash all my sins away.
Washed all my sins away, washed all my sins away;
And there have I, though vile as he, washed all my sins
    away...

The blood of Christ sets humankind free from all bondage. Because our chains are gone, we can walk in freedom. In these days we will see a radical return to the message of the redemptive blood of Christ, *knowing* that we are not redeemed with silver and gold, but with the precious blood of Christ. Jesus declared, *"You shall know the truth and the truth shall make you free"* (John 8:32). With that in mind, we must spend time daily meditating upon the Word of God, letting it get deep within our souls. Only then will we experience its transforming effects of soul revival, wisdom, joy, and insight (see Ps. 19:7-14). Since knowing the truth in our hearts sets us free, the question must be asked, *Why are so many believers living in different levels of bondage and defeat?* One of the greatest reasons is that we have left our first love.

### Nothing But the Blood
*Robert Lowry (1826-1899)*

What can wash away my sin?
Nothing but the blood of Jesus;
What can make me whole again?
Nothing but the blood of Jesus.

*Refrain*
Oh! Precious is the flow
That makes me white as snow;
No other fount I know,
Nothing but the blood of Jesus.

For my pardon, this I see,
Nothing but the blood of Jesus;
For my cleansing this my plea,
Nothing but the blood of Jesus.

Nothing can for sin atone,
Nothing but the blood of Jesus;
Naught of good that I have done,
Nothing but the blood of Jesus.

This is all my hope and peace,
Nothing but the blood of Jesus;
This is all my righteousness,
Nothing but the blood of Jesus.

Now by this I'll overcome—
Nothing but the blood of Jesus,
Now by this I'll reach my home—
Nothing but the blood of Jesus.

Glory! Glory! This I sing—
Nothing but the blood of Jesus,
All my praise for this I bring—
Nothing but the blood of Jesus.

We must let these words become a searchlight, scanning
the deepest confines of our hearts. These words were written
so many years ago; yet their probing power is still vital for
today, even in our hi-tech and fast-paced world. Here's just
the first verse of another hymn that speaks so poignantly:

**Alas! And Did My Savior Bleed?**
*Isaac Watts (1707)*

Alas! And did my Savior bleed
And did my Sovereign die?
Would He devote that sacred head
For sinners such as I?

The point is this: All that Christ did, He did because of His great redemptive love for us.

## OBEDIENCE IS BETTER

Our prayer must be, "Lord, restore my passion for Jesus." The blood of Christ has provided us with overwhelming victory. We do not have to continue living in defeat; however, it will require our persistent commitment to overcome the strongholds. If we will dedicate ourselves to Him again and resolve to obey Him, this can change; we can start walking in lifelong victory.

The great and precious old hymn, "Trust and Obey" states:

Trust and obey,

For there is no other way

To be happy in Jesus,

But to trust and obey.

This is one of the most important aspects of the Christian walk—learning how to quickly obey the voice of the Spirit of God. We must never run from God, but to Him. He longs to help us, not hurt us. He has promised to never leave us, to live in us, and to always be with us, and because He is always with us, we are assured of the overwhelming victory. As Deuteronomy says:

> *Be strong and of good courage, do not fear nor be afraid of them; for the LORD your God, He is the One who goes with you. He will not leave you nor forsake you* (Deut. 31:6).

## SURRENDER TO HIS WILL

The word *obey* is one of the strongest words in the English language; it deals with the surrender of one's will to the desire of another. Jesus' prayer in His last hours of freedom showed true obedience and surrender: *"Father, if it is Your will, take this cup away from Me; nevertheless not My will, but Yours, be done"* (Luke 22:42). True faith is always evidenced by obedience, which is why the word in the New Testament that is usually translated "faith" also means "faithfulness." True faithfulness in our lives is evidenced by obedience to His voice, and it is one of the main mandates that the Lord gave to us in Matthew 6:33-34:

> But seek first the kingdom of God and His righteousness, and all these things shall be added to you. Therefore do not worry about tomorrow, for tomorrow will worry about its own things...

Many Christians appear to be as mixed-up as a termite in a yo-yo; this confusion is most certainly fostered by the foe of our souls, as we know that God is not the author of confusion (see 1 Cor. 14:33). Sadly, many saints have spent too much of their lives in disorientation and defeat because they have not obeyed the Word of God. It is as we seek first the desire of the King and the advancing of His Kingdom that we will receive clear guidance.

## SEEK HIS KINGDOM FIRST

One source of confusion is that many are walking "in the light of their own sparks" and not in the revealed light of God's Word. They have made vital decisions based on their own desires and other earthly, temporary matters, rather than seeking first the purposes of God's Kingdom. If they had based all of their decisions on the purposes of His Kingdom first, everything else would have been added to them. If our lives are based on God's plans and desires, we will have nothing to be anxious about—we will know our true source and protector.

There is no greater freedom, no greater peace, than that

which is the result of living our lives dedicated to the Lord in all things. We are being given another chance to do this now. Let's not let this year pass like the others. We are created to be the leading, thinking head—not the following, uninformed tail. God's plan is for us to be above and not below. Now is the time for us to walk in peace and freedom.

# CHAPTER 9
## *Unction to Function*

The Lord never requires anything of us that He does not equip us to do. And to fulfill our mission and commission as believers, we need His anointing. Truly, we can do nothing without it. Actually, Jesus said, *"Without Me you can do nothing"* (John 15:5b), but because the anointing is so inseparably attached to Christ, the meaning is the same. The anointing represents the indwelling presence and power of the Lord, without which we truly can do nothing of lasting significance or value in the Kingdom of God. It doesn't matter how gifted we are, how talented we are, how athletic we are, or how intelligent or well-educated we are. Without Him, we can do nothing.

*"Without Me you can do nothing."* The first time I read that, I felt insulted. Then I thought, *Well, maybe I don't understand what He means by nothing.* So I looked up the Greek word for *nothing* and really got blown away. In Greek, the word for *nothing (oudeis)*, means, well—"nothing." Nada. Zilch. Absolute zero with a vacuum in the middle of it. As a matter of fact, if any word can mean "less than nothing," *oudeis* is that word. Jesus was saying, in other words, that apart from

Him, apart from His divine touch on all that we say and do, our lives will accomplish absolutely, totally nothing.

However, lest we become discouraged over this, we need to remember that as believers we have Christ Himself living in us through His Holy Spirit. And the Christ who said, *"Without Me you can do nothing,"* is the same Christ through whom we can do all things as He strengthens us (see Phil. 4:13). By ourselves we can do nothing, but with His anointing, we can change the world!

This is why, if we want to walk in the anointing of God, we must become completely dependent upon the Holy Spirit. We were created for fellowship with God, to walk with Him and partner with Him in exercising dominion over the created order. The happiest people I know are those who are walking under the canopy of God. I have never met people more contented and gratified than those who are walking under the destiny of God for their lives. We need the anointing because without it we cannot fulfill our full destiny in Christ.

We need the anointing because we have been commissioned to do the works of Christ. Jesus said, *"Most assuredly, I say to you, he who believes in Me, the works that I do he will do also; and greater works than these he will do, because I go to My Father"* (John 14:12). Our Lord has commissioned us to do a wonderful task, but He doesn't expect us to do it without His touch. In fact, it would be unjust and unfair of Him to give us an assignment without an anointing, a task without His empowering touch.

Many Christians, unfortunately, either out of ignorance or out of eagerness to be about the Lord's work, rush out without seeking or waiting for His anointing, and then they wonder why they see few results. That's not the Lord's way. He will never set us about the task He has given us without first placing that touch of Heaven on our lives. And more often than not, receiving that touch is a matter of waiting on Him.

Ponder this powerful promise found in Isaiah 40:31:

*But those who wait on the Lord shall renew their strength; they shall mount up with wings like eagles, they shall run and not be weary, they shall walk and not faint.*

Clearly, we need the anointing of the Lord! And the good news is, any one of us who wants it can receive it. I've said it many times before, and I'll say it again because many Christians still have trouble really, truly believing it: The anointing is not for Christian "superstars"; it is for every believer. In reality, there are no Christian "superstars." There may be some self-righteous "fat cats" who think they are God's greatest gift to the Church, but God thinks differently. Anyone who is full of himself or herself has no room for the anointing. In fact, God said He resists the proud, but gives great grace to the humble (see 1 Pet. 5:5). The only "superstar" is the One who made the stars, the Word who was in the beginning, who was with God and who was God (see John 1:1). It is in Christ Jesus that the fullness of the Godhead dwells (see Col. 2:9-10), and our highest goal must be to point hurting desperate humanity to Christ the Healer.

Recently, the Lord spoke these sobering words to me, saying, "The highest form of treason and treachery is to take the gifts He gives us to woo the Bride to Him and use these gifts to woo the Bride to ourselves." We must set our hearts to never fall into this type of ministry. This is why God loves to use the humble and the broken; they are the ones who have no illusions about themselves. They know they are nothing without Him. But with Him and by Him, all things are possible.

## THINK BIGGER

It is time for us to think big and to believe big, following Paul's instructions found in Ephesians 3:20-21:

*Now to Him who is able to do exceedingly abundantly above all that we ask or think, according to the power that works in us, to Him be glory in the church by Christ Jesus to all generations, forever and ever. Amen.*

Recently, while on a hunting trip in the beautiful, deep East Texas woods, I had a powerful prophetic encounter with Christ Jesus. I had made my way deep into the woods and was sitting on the ground, resting against a massive oak tree. The setting was like something out of a novel. The early sun was warmly filtering down through the giant canopy of color, the leaves were exquisite with brilliant fall foliage, and the woods were extremely quite except for the sounds of nature. In the distance, high in the sky, I heard the alluring honking of the Canadian geese as they made their pilgrimage south. I listened, delighted, to the wonderful sounds of the birds— the cardinal singing its song and the chickadee chirping. In the nearby tree, I could hear the sound of a small squirrel scurrying from limb to limb, enjoying the bountiful harvest of nuts. I was so enjoying the peaceful quietness far removed from the hustle and bustle of airports, freeways, cell phones, schedules, and so forth.

Then, from the top of the tree that I was reclining against, I heard the sound of a small marble-sized acorn falling down through the tree branches. Eventually, it fell softly on my leg, coming to rest near my foot. The Lord Jesus said to me, "Pick it up!" When I picked up the small, brown acorn, the Lord asked me this question, "What is that in your hand?"

Somewhat confused by the simplistic question, I replied, "It is an acorn!"

Then, in a most instructive tone, Christ said to me, "Strange. You see only a small acorn, but I see a whole forest!"

At that statement, my entire being was electrified with such a feeling of excitement and expectation, knowing that God's plans and purposes are so much bigger than we realize. Then, in a wonderful encounter, He began to instruct me concerning humanity's propensity to underestimate what we have been given, stressing that we must enlarge our thinking and our concept of His ability. He encouraged me to believe Him for bigger things and to never forget that He has blessed us with all spiritual blessings.

Here's an acrostic for *blessed* that will encourage us all:

**B**elieve in God's goodness, regardless of circumstances (see Nah. 1:7)

**L**et go of agendas, allowing God to plan better lives for us (see Jer. 29:11)

**E**mbrace reality by accepting the truth of our lives and letting God use them for His glory (see Rom. 8:32)

**S**ee from God's heart by training ourselves to view life from the Kingdom perspective (see Rom. 8:37).

**S**tay where we are while holding on to our faith and dependence on His providence (see Heb. 10:35).

**E**xpect to be blessed, looking for and receiving God's fulfillment on a daily basis (see Ps. 121:1-2)

**D**edicate it all to Christ, living for the one who died for us (see Matt. 6:33)

The Bible informs us that, on the Day of Pentecost, the Holy Spirit came down and filled *all* who were in that upper room (see Acts 2:4)—not just the apostles and not just the men, but everyone in the room was filled with the Holy Spirit. Everyone in that room then poured out onto the streets of Jerusalem, speaking in other tongues and boldly proclaiming the gospel of Christ. Here we find a critical key. The Spirit of God gives us the anointing, not so that we can get a chill down our spines, but so that we can proclaim the Word of God with boldness and power. It is amazing how God opens doors for us to share His message of redemption.

Once I spoke at a wonderful church near Washington, D.C., and after the service, the pastor and his wife took me to dinner. It was one of those fancy restaurants that require advance reservations and that employ several nicely-dressed young women as hostesses to seat the guests—a really first-class dining establishment. As one of these young hostesses led us to our table, the Lord said to me, "I want to win her to me."

I could already sense somehow that this young woman was very cold and hostile toward the gospel, so I said to God, "Lord, I don't think she's ready to hear much right now."

"But I am ready to win her to Me," He replied.

I knew better than to argue with the Lord, but all through the meal, I kept wondering how God was going to reach this hostile woman and bring her to Himself. As we got ready to leave, the pastor paid the check, and we started out through the same door by which we had entered. Once again the Lord spoke to me: "I still want to win her."

"How, Lord?" I asked.

He replied, "Ask her about the spider web tattoo around her belly button with the black widow spider crawling toward it."

I have to admit that I felt a little awkward. The pastor and wife, who were my hosts, were elegant, dignified people who probably were not very familiar with tattoos and such or with this kind of working of the Lord, and I was afraid the whole situation would be an embarrassment to them and perhaps to me as well. Nevertheless, I called them over to me and shared what the Lord had said He wanted to do, hoping to prepare them for it. When I said that the Lord wanted to win that young woman to Him, the pastor said, "Oh, delightful!"

But as I told them what I had been shown about the spider web tattoo, he said, "Really!" and his wife's eyes got big and round. Then he asked, "What are we going to do?"

I said, "We're going to go over there and ask her about it." What else could we do? The Lord had made His will clear; we could either obey or not. So we walked over to the same hostess who had seated us earlier, and I said to her, "I just wanted to tell you that Jesus Christ is the Son of God, and He loves you dearly." Her eyes just sort of glazed over, as if she was trying to tune me out. I took a deep breath and pressed on. "He's going to do something for you that'll show you just how much He loves you. God has a plan for your life. He just showed me something about you, and the only reason He did it was because He wants so much for you to be saved." She eyed me warily. Then I said to her, "I don't know you. We've never met before, have we?"

"No," she replied, "We've never met."

"Let me ask you a question. Do you have a tattoo of a spider web with a black widow crawling toward your belly button?"

Her eyes grew wide, her mouth fell open, and she screamed, "I can't believe this!" Then she flipped up the bottom of her shirt and, sure enough, there was the web and spider tattoo. She was completely disarmed. All her defenses and hostility evaporated, and she began crying. This God who knew all about her also knew she was ready to open her heart. The pastor and his wife then led her to Christ right there! Some months later, I made a return visit to that church, and guess who I saw sitting there in that sanctuary? That's right. The girl with the tattoo. Isn't God amazing?

## ANOTHER TATTOO STORY

Here's another tattoo story that turns out to be an encouraging report! I was traveling and extremely busy, seeking to keep up with the commitments I had made for ministry meetings. Rushing to get to the gate to catch the next plane for the last segment of my trip, I arrived just in time to hear the announcement, "Due to maintenance problems, this flight had been delayed!"

Extremely put out and disappointed, I called the people I was supposed to be traveling to meet, and I explained to them about my delay and that I would be on a later plane. Afterward, I went into the nearby bar and ordered some sparkling water. As I was sitting there, trying to catch up on e-mails, I looked to my left and saw, four stools over, a young lady who looked about twenty years old. She was hunched over a huge margarita, and I thought to myself, *Man, that thing is big enough to bathe a huge dog in.* Then I looked up and, with shock, noticed that the young lady had a big black tattoo on her face—not something nice, but something that looked like Mike Tyson's tattoo. Without realizing it, I was staring at the tattoo. Suddenly, the young lady said to me in a very hostile tone, "What the blank are you looking at?" I'm sure she thought her vulgarity and hostility would offend me.

Without hesitation I said "You!" Then these words came out of my mouth, "If you will come over here and sit down, I will tell you why you are hiding behind this mask." Suddenly, she scooted over to sit beside me, and her whole demeanor changed.

God began to reveal to me the deep wounds within her life, the bitter betrayal and horrible abuse of a father. As I shared with her what God was showing me, she began weeping and gasping, and her heart was wide open to receive Christ the King. I explained to her the simple gospel and the redemptive love of Jesus and then asked if she would like to receive Jesus as her Savior. She prayed this simple prayer: "Lord Jesus, please come into my heart and forgive me of my sins and save me!" At that moment, her face brightened. She had a beaming smile and a bright twinkle in her eyes as she screamed, grabbing me around my neck, "He did! He did!"

"How do you know?" I asked.

"I can feel Him in my heart!" she exclaimed. Tears streamed down her tattooed face as she said a heartfelt thank you.

I said, "Let's thank Jesus! He deserves the glory."

Soon, I was on a plane on my way to a distant city to minister that night to a civic center packed full of people who were hungry to hear about God's power and plan for their lives. Sitting in my seat over 30,000 feet above the ground, my heart was overflowing and rejoicing, knowing that God cares for everyone, even a lonely, misguided, brokenhearted, wayward young tattooed girl. I love it when God shows up and shows off! The truth is, the early Church preached with signs and wonders, and we should do the same thing.

I love it when God reveals those sorts of things about people. He does it because He is after their hearts, and He wants to draw them out of spiritual darkness and into the light of His eternal love. Peter wrote that the Lord is *"not willing that any should perish but that all should come to repentance"* (2 Pet. 3:9b). Likewise, Paul said that God *"desires all men to be saved and to come to the knowledge of the truth"* (1 Tim. 2:4).

This doesn't mean that everyone will be saved. God's *desire* is for everyone to be saved, but only those who hear and respond to the gospel message will be saved. That's where we come in as believers. Paul said:

> For *"whoever calls on the name of the Lord shall be saved." How then shall they call on Him in whom they have not believed? And how shall they believe in Him of whom they have not heard? And how shall they hear without a preacher? And how shall they preach unless they are sent?...So then faith comes by hearing, and hearing by the word of God* (Rom. 10:13-15,17).

# CHAPTER 10
## *Empowerment*

As I already discussed in the last chapter, without Christ Jesus and His anointing, we can do nothing. Let's look at a story from some men who did not understand this principal. They learned a huge lesson as a result of stepping out without the anointing:

*Now God worked unusual miracles by the hands of Paul, so that even handkerchiefs or aprons were brought from his body to the sick, and the diseases left them and the evil spirits went out of them. Then some of the itinerant Jewish exorcists took it upon themselves to call the name of the Lord Jesus over those who had evil spirits, saying, "We exorcise you by the Jesus whom Paul preaches." Also there were seven sons of Sceva, a Jewish chief priest, who did so. And the evil spirit answered and said, "Jesus I know, and Paul I know; but who are you?" Then the man in whom the evil spirit was leaped on them, overpowered them, and prevailed against them, so that they fled out of that house naked and wounded. This became known both to all Jews and Greeks dwelling in Ephesus; and fear fell on them all, and the name of the Lord Jesus was magnified* (Acts 19:11-17).

Sceva's seven boys thought that all they needed to cast out demons was to invoke the name of "Jesus whom Paul preaches." They didn't even preach in the name of Jesus themselves, yet they thought they could appropriate His power. They found out differently when the demonized man they were trying to deliver overpowered them and "tanned their hides!" There is no such thing as second-hand anointing.

Does the anointing really make a difference? Just ask Simon Peter. The big, rough, and impetuous fisherman was a man of great courage whose heart was in the right place, but whose impulsiveness sometimes affected his judgment. The most famous instance of this happened in the Garden of Gethsemane, when Peter single-handedly took on a whole mob of soldiers and temple police sent to arrest Jesus, attacking them with a single dikara—an 18-inch-long short sword. Had Jesus not stopped him, there would have been a lot more blood shed than just the severed ear of Malchus, the high priest's slave (see John 18:1-12).

Yet just a few hours later, during Jesus' trial, "fearless" Peter was left quaking in his sandals when a servant girl in the high priest's household accused him of being one of Jesus' men. He denied it. In fact, over the course of maybe two hours, Peter denied Jesus three times, each time more vehemently than before. The third time, he even threw in a couple of curses to be even more convincing (see Matt. 26:69-75; Mark 14:66-72; Luke 22:54-62; John 18:15-27). Obviously, courage alone was not enough.

Fast-forward about fifty-three days to the day of Pentecost. Peter was one of the 120 newly Spirit-filled believers who streamed out of that upper room, and he stood up and boldly and publicly preached Christ in a powerful sermon that brought 3,000 new believers into the Kingdom of God. From then on, and for the rest of his life, Peter was steadfast, not only in courage, but also in spiritual power.

What changed? What happened in Peter's heart? Acts 1:8 happened. Just before He ascended into Heaven, Jesus promised His disciples:

*You shall receive power when the Holy Spirit has come upon you; and you shall be witnesses to Me in Jerusalem, and in all Judea and Samaria, and to the end of the earth* (Acts 1:8).

Ten days later, that promise was fulfilled at Pentecost. What happened to change Peter's life? The anointing happened. The anointing transformed Simon Peter from a guy who couldn't stay stuck to a man who preached the boldest, most powerful sermon in history. And 3,000 souls are in Heaven today because of it.

# CHAPTER 11
## *Anointing and Authority*

As we saw in the previous chapter, the anointing took away Peter's instability. It took away his fear of people. It firmly anchored his faith and thoroughly grounded his love for Christ. When Peter spoke to the crowd of onlookers in Jerusalem that day, he pulled no punches, but was extremely bold and exceeding brave:

> *Men of Israel, hear these words: Jesus of Nazareth, a Man attested by God to you by miracles, wonders, and signs which God did through Him in your midst, as you yourselves also know—Him, being delivered by the determined purpose and foreknowledge of God, you have taken by lawless hands, have crucified, and put to death; whom God raised up, having loosed the pains of death, because it was not possible that He should be held by it... Therefore let all the house of Israel know assuredly that God has made this Jesus, whom you crucified, both Lord and Christ* (Acts 2:22-24,36).

Are these the words of a man who was trying to impress people because he was afraid of what they would think of him? No. He was under the anointing now. He was not afraid to stand up or speak out. He was not afraid of what people could do to him. His only concern was to bear faithful witness to his Lord. We too need the anointing that rested on Peter to rest on us so that our tongues will be loosed, as his was, and so that we will stand up and boldly bear witness in both word and action, just as he did.

Many of us today do not speak boldly because we are afraid of offending people or turning them away. Lost people need to be confronted with the truth in a straightforward but compassionate manner. Peter certainly did not coddle his listeners. He told them what they needed to hear, and his words had a powerful effect

> *Now when they heard this, they were cut to the heart, and said to Peter and the rest of the apostles, "Men and brethren, what shall we do?" Then Peter said to them, "Repent, and let every one of you be baptized in the name of Jesus Christ for the remission of sins; and you shall receive the gift of the Holy Spirit. For the promise is to you and to your children, and to all who are afar off, as many as the Lord our God will call." And with many other words he testified and exhorted them, saying, "Be saved from this perverse generation." Then those who gladly received his word were baptized; and that day about three thousand souls were added to them* (Acts 2:37-41).

Peter's listeners were "cut to the heart" under the conviction of the Holy Spirit. The Greek word for cut, *katanusso*, means to "pierce thoroughly," to "agitate violently," and to "prick." It means they were slashed to the very center of their souls. Does that sound "seeker-friendly"? Not to our modern ears. But in reality, it is seeker-friendly because seekers need to hear a gospel that will slash them to the very center of their souls so that they will be moved to repent of their sins and trust Christ. Part of the problem with much of the Church today is that we have drifted far away from preaching a gospel that makes people conform to it. Instead, we mold and conform the gospel we preach to appeal to and appease the minds and hearts of wicked people. That's why we so desperately need the anointing. The anointing will bring us back to the heart of the gospel. The anointing will bring lost people face-to-face with a God whom they can no longer ignore, whom they must make a decision about.

The power of the anointing is found not in what we "do," but in holy living, since we are confident that Christ has already done all the work for us on the cross. His work of redemption on the cross is a finished work. All we have to do is step into Him and invite Him to step into us. As Paul said, *"For to me, to live is Christ, and to die is gain"* (Phil. 1:21). We let Christ live His life through us. It is a yielded life, a surrendered life, a life free from the fear or worry of having to do enough to please God and earn His favor. As His beloved and anointed children by faith, we already have His favor.

Paul tells us in Ephesians:

> *For by grace you have been saved through faith, and that not of yourselves; it is the gift of God, not of works, lest anyone should boast. For we are His workmanship, created in Christ Jesus for good works, which God prepared beforehand that we should walk in them* (Eph. 2:8-10).

See, it's not about what we have done, but what He has done. Our part is to place our lives completely and totally in His hands, saying, "Here I am, Lord! Anoint me! Live your life through me." And He will. He will take what we yield to Him. That's what the anointing is all about.

## AVAILABLE TO ALL BELIEVERS

*All* believers can receive the power and anointing. God plays no favorites; the ground is level at the foot of the cross. All believers, without exception, come to Christ through repentance of sin and faith in the one who covered their sins with His blood. And without exception, all believers have the same access to the presence and power of the Lord. The difference between those believers who receive and walk in the anointing and those who do not is, as we have already seen, a matter of hunger. Those who receive the anointing are those individuals who are hungry enough to pursue it.

Hunger is the critical key, but motivation is important also. We must consider these questions: *Why do we want the anointing? Do we want it for ourselves, for our own personal enjoyment or benefit, or do we want it so we can help others? Are we after our own glory, or do we seek to glorify God?* When Jesus spoke the words recorded in Luke 4:18-19, which we looked at earlier, He was in the synagogue in His hometown of Nazareth, reading from the prophet Isaiah. Putting those words into their larger context reveals the purpose of the anointing both for Jesus and for us:

> *The Spirit of the Lord God is upon Me, because the Lord has anointed Me to preach good tidings to the poor; He has sent Me to heal the brokenhearted, to proclaim liberty to the captives, and the opening of the prison to those who are bound; to proclaim the acceptable year of the Lord, and the day of vengeance of our God; to comfort all who mourn, to console those who mourn in Zion, to give them beauty for ashes, the oil of joy for mourning, the garment of praise for the spirit of heaviness; that they may be called trees of righteousness, the planting of the Lord, that **He may be glorified** (Isa. 61:1-3).*

*"That He may be glorified"*—that is the reason for the anointing. When God is glorified, people turn to Him. When Christ is lifted up, people are saved. As Jesus Himself said, *"And I, if I am lifted up from the earth, will draw all peoples to Myself"* (John 12:32). When the gospel of Christ is preached in the power of the anointing, lives are changed and destinies are altered forever. Dead religion is supplanted by vibrant, living relationship with the living God. Every eye is focused on the Lord. If our heart-desire is to glorify the Lord, to exalt His name before people, and to see the lost come to Christ, then our hearts are in the right posture to receive and walk in the anointing.

Jesus' mission on earth was to preach the good news, heal the brokenhearted, liberate those in spiritual bondage, and comfort the mourning, replacing their sorrow with joy. As His friends and followers, we have the same mission. Some may think, *But I'm not a preacher,* or *I'm not a counselor.* That's OK. We can all be a friend. Many people today pass each day in crushing loneliness. They need friends who will care about them and take a genuine interest in them as people who have hopes and dreams, joys and sorrows. Being a friend does not require any special training. All it takes is a sensitive and compassionate heart.

## CAN YOU HEAR THE SOUND?

The Lord Jesus spoke these words to me, saying, "Bobby, on earth these sounds are almost muted; however, in Heaven they are amplified!"

I questioned, "Lord, what sounds?"

He replied, "The sound of the breaking of a heart and the shattering of dreams!"

My heart was so stirred by His words, knowing I have been guilty of not taking the time to be sensitive to the sounds of hurting people. I began to pray "Lord, open my heart that I might feel, and open my eyes that I might see."

Let's consider who we can be a friend to today. Who can we encourage with a kind or comforting word? Who can we pray for or with? Opportunities to bless others and to glorify Christ are all around us. All we have to do is look.

# CHAPTER 12

## *Ordinary People, Extraordinary Empowerment*

**M**any Christians assume that the anointing normally manifests in extraordinary ways and situations. In reality, the anointing usually operates best in the most ordinary of circumstances. One day, Peter and John were on their way to the temple when they saw a man crippled from birth sitting by the temple gate called Beautiful, begging for alms. There was nothing extraordinary in that; beggars were common in Jerusalem, and this man had begged at this same gate every day for years. It was a day like any other, except for the anointing of the Lord, which was about to touch this man and change his life forever. When he saw Peter and John about to enter the temple, he asked for alms.

*And fixing his eyes on him, with John, Peter said, "Look at us." So he gave them his attention, expecting to receive something from them. Then Peter said, "Silver and gold I do not have, but what I do have I give you: In the name of Jesus Christ of Nazareth, rise up and walk." And he took him by the right hand and lifted him up, and immediately his feet and ankle bones received strength. So he, leaping up, stood and walked and entered the temple with them—walking, leaping, and praising God. And all the people saw him walking and praising God. Then they knew that it was he who sat begging alms at the Beautiful Gate of the temple; and they were filled with wonder and amazement at what had happened to him* (Acts 3:4-10).

Peter and John probably did not go to the temple with the deliberate intention of healing a crippled beggar, but in the daily course of life, they saw a need and addressed it. That's how the anointing works best, with no fanfare and in response to needs and opportunities that cross our paths. It is also the way Jesus operated. He steadfastly refused to produce signs or miracles on demand, but always responded to a simple, humble cry for help.

The healing of the crippled beggar occurred with no fanfare, but the result certainly drew a crowd. Walking unassisted on his own two feet for the first time in his life, the beggar entered the temple with Peter and John, *"walking, leaping, and praising God."* It was the ninth hour, the hour of prayer at the temple. Imagine how his joyous entrance must have broken up the prayer service! A crowd quickly gathered. Seeing his opportunity, Peter flowed with the anointing:

*Now as the lame man who was healed held on to Peter and John, all the people ran together to them in the porch which is called Solomon's, greatly amazed. So when Peter saw it, he responded to the people: "Men of Israel, why do you marvel at this? Or why look so intently at us, as though by our own power or godliness we had made this man walk? The God of Abraham, Isaac, and Jacob, the God of our fathers, glorified His Servant Jesus, whom you delivered up and denied in the presence of Pilate, when he was determined to let Him go. But you denied the Holy One and the Just, and asked for a murderer to be granted to you, and killed the Prince of life, whom God raised from the dead, of which we are witnesses. And His name, through faith in His name, has made this man strong, whom you see and know. Yes, the faith which comes through Him has given him this perfect soundness in the presence of you all"* (Acts 3:11-16).

Peter and John were ordinary men—fishermen—who had been touched by God in an extraordinary way to do extraordinary deeds for His glory. They were ordinary men who walked in an extraordinary anointing. And they were quick to give credit where credit was due. Peter used this occasion of the healing of a crippled beggar to give glory to God and to proclaim Christ to those in the temple, some of whom, at least, had clamored for Jesus' death not many weeks before.

God likes to anoint ordinary people because He knows they won't try to take the glory for themselves. In the power and flow of the anointing, we must always direct the gaze of others to the Lord. The moment we try to point to ourselves, we step out of God's will and shut ourselves off from the flow. Always, always, always we must point to Christ. He is our joy, our strength, our destiny. And He is the hope of the nations. The Spirit of the Lord is upon us. And God has anointed us—you and me—for these very days that we are living in. No previous generation has had the opportunity that we have to impact the world with the gospel of Jesus Christ. He has called, commissioned, and anointed us to do His works—and even greater works—in the earth so that multitudes will be drawn to Him. God has anointed us. Now what will we do?

Recently, I was at a meeting where I ministered on healing and the power of Jesus to still accomplish supernatural miracles today. After the service was over, as I was making my way out of the meeting area, a sweet lady stopped me. For over an hour, I had been speaking about God's power to heal and the fact that the supernatural is available for us today. She questioned, almost in a mocking and skeptical tone, "Well, why don't Jesus heal my hand?" She extended her right hand, and I was stunned to see that it was extremely maimed. Her fingers twisted and deformed so much that it did not even look like a hand.

These words almost shot from my lips as I grasped her mangled hand in mine, "Well, why don't *He!*" No sooner had these words came from my mouth, than her fingers began to pop and snap and twist, and in an instant, her right hand was totally restored.

In a second, she was crying and screaming, "He did! He did!"

I replied, "Yes, He did!" Even if we are weak in our faith, Jesus is still powerful and loving, and He longs for us to experience His goodness.

## ANOTHER STORY

While I was ministering at a church in Ohio, I was at the book table having a book signing. A family came forward, and as I was signing their book, I noticed that the man had a huge bandage on his hand. So I asked, "What's wrong with your hand?"

He said, in an embarrassed tone, "I cut my finger off!"

Suddenly I said, almost in a joking tone, "Well, you know Jesus has original parts." And I said a quick prayer, "Lord, heal him!"

They moved on, and someone else was standing in front of me. A few months later, I was back in the same location in Ohio, and once again I was at the book table signing books. The same lady came forward, and she said, "I want to tell you what happened to my husband's finger." She told me that when they got home that night, he said to her, "Honey, my finger feels funny." She said to me, "Bobby, I am a nurse at the hospital, and I was the one who put his bandage on, so I thought it must be too tight." She undid the bandage, only to discover that the finger that had been cut off in the accident with the carpenter saw was completely restored. There was not even a sign of a scar. Together, she and I rejoiced at what Jesus had done. Truly, God can do anything (see Gen. 18:14).

# CHAPTER 13

## *Receiving Divine Empowerment*

Only those who are truly hungry and thirsty for the things of God will receive the anointing because they are the only ones desperate enough to pursue it. That's how I received the anointing. I was so desperate for "something more" that it brought me to a crisis point in my ministry. Let me tell you about it.

I remember standing before our church family in First Baptist Church of Bullard, Texas, and saying, "If this is all there is to the ministry, I am through with it." I was sick and tired of hearing people say the days of miracles had passed and that Jesus no longer healed and delivered. I could no longer explain away such verses as Mark 16:17-18, *"And these signs will follow those who believe: In My name they will cast out demons...they will lay hands on the sick, and they will recover."*

I am a realist. I feel we must do what the Bible teaches. We are to be *"doers of the word, and not hearers only..."* (James 1:22). I became very dissatisfied with the emptiness and lack of power that I was experiencing in my life and seeing in the lives of all the pastors I knew. I had not experienced the anointing Jesus said I could and should have as a believer. As a result, I became hungry and desperate for more of God. *"As the deer pants for the water brooks, so pants my soul for You, O God. My soul thirsts for God, for the living God. When shall I come and appear before God?"* (Ps. 42:1-2). I found myself like David, when he cried out,

> *O God, You are my God; early will I seek You; my soul thirsts for You; my flesh longs for You in a dry and thirsty land where there is no water. So I have looked for You in the sanctuary, to see Your power and Your glory* (Ps. 63:1-2).

I began to cry out for God to fill this hunger, and I became desperate for the power of God to be demonstrated in my life for His glory. The Lord then began to speak to me and give me promises—such as Isaiah 43:19-21:

> *Behold, I will do a new thing, now it shall spring forth; shall you not know it? I will even make a road in the wilderness and rivers in the desert.... I give waters in the wilderness and rivers in the desert, to give to My people, My chosen. This people I have formed for Myself; they shall declare My praise.*

God said He would open up for me rivers in the desert. Well, I was sure in a desert—a place that is dry and barren. Yet God is so very, very faithful and merciful. He will never forsake those who are truly hungry and thirsty. As He promised through Isaiah:

> *For I will pour water on him who is thirsty, and floods on the dry ground; I will pour My Spirit on your descendants, and My blessing on your offspring; they will spring up among the grass like willows by the watercourses* (Isa. 44:3-4).

I began to pray and seek God. I could not go on without the power that Jesus had promised me in His Word. *"Behold,*

*I give you the authority to trample on serpents and scorpions, and over all the power of the enemy, and nothing shall by any means hurt you"* (Luke 10:19). The Holy Spirit continually brought this Scripture before me, and I was sick of the world mocking and scoffing the Church of Jesus Christ, saying, "Where is your God?"

One Sunday in October, 1989, I had an extremely busy and trying schedule. My day was as full as it could get. I was scheduled to preach twice on Sunday morning, then go to Rock Hill Baptist Church, thirty miles away, and preach a funeral service at 2:00 p.m., and then come back to First Baptist Church in Bullard for our twenty-fifth wedding anniversary reception at 3:30 p.m., and then preach two more times that night. As I was returning from the funeral service, the Holy Spirit spoke to my heart and said, "As your day is, so will your strength be."

I wasn't sure exactly what He meant, but I said, "It sounds good to me!"

In the service that evening, my wife Carolyn was sitting next to me before I was to preach. I knew she was very tired and exhausted from all of her hard work and the hectic schedule she had been keeping, so I just placed my hand on the back of her neck and was softly praying for God to give her strength. She took my hand away and said, "Bobby, your hand is so very warm. It is like an electric heating pad on my back." Then she said, "I feel great. Do you think you should offer to pray for anyone else who might need refreshing and healing?" So I invited people to come forward who wanted prayer, and as I lifted my hand to pray for them, the power and presence of the Holy Spirit overcame them, and many simply fell over under God's power. When they got up, they were refreshed and some were healed. This was one of the first times that God demonstrated His power in my life.

A few months later, Benny Hinn came to a nearby church. God told me that if I would go and have him lay hands on me, I would receive the same anointing that is upon his life. At that time, I didn't know anything about Benny Hinn or the mighty miracle ministry that God had given to him. After Benny Hinn had ministered, he sat down on the platform, and as another person stood to speak, God said, "Bobby, I want you to get up out of your seat and walk up to Brother Benny Hinn and tell him what I have told you about him laying hands upon you so you will receive the anointing upon your life that I've placed upon him." So I did.

Not one person tried to stop me. Men parted in front of me like the Red Sea parted in front of Moses. I came to Benny Hinn and explained to him why I had come. He looked intently into my eyes and said, "Put your hand on the back of my neck." He prayed for me and laid his hands upon me, and the Holy Spirit placed an anointing upon my life. I will never be the same. Since then, God has opened great doors of opportunity for Carolyn and me to go all over the United States and other countries to carry our Demonstrations of God's Power Miracle Crusades.

God wants to anoint all of us. He desires to raise up many little, unknown, insignificant nobodies, like Bobby Conner, to shake nations so that Jesus Christ will get the glory. It is not our wisdom, strength, or position that will make the world take notice; it is the anointing of God.

*For you see your calling, brethren, that not many wise according to the flesh, not many mighty, not many noble, are called. But God has chosen the foolish things of the world to put to shame the wise, and God has chosen the weak things of the world to put to shame the things which are mighty; and the base things of the world and the things which are despised God has chosen, and the things which are not, to bring to nothing the things that are, that no flesh should glory in His presence* (1 Cor. 1:26-29).

We can be very sure that there will be no superstars in this great move of God's Spirit—only Jesus will get the glory and the honor. If we are hungry and humble, God will anoint us. Let's ask God to place a real hunger for His holiness and for His anointing in our hearts. If we get desperate and thirsty enough, we will receive a fresh anointing.

# CHAPTER 14
## *Fresh Oil Produces Fresh Fire*

I've always liked fast cars. My first car was a 1949 Ford with a V8 motor, but it just was not fast enough. So I had that motor removed and put a 1957 Oldsmobile huge horsepower V8 in. I loved the way it would fly. Later, I got a 1957 two-door hard top Chevy with a souped-up V8 with a full race cam. It was the fastest car in the region. When I surrendered to preach, I had a '68 GTO. It had a 441 cubic inch engine with two factory-installed four-barrel carburetors and a hydro-stick. At the time, it was the fastest car you could buy off the showroom floor. Man, I loved that car! You might ask, "What's that got to do with my need of the anointing?" Don't worry; I am getting to it.

Today, if I wanted a fast car, I might go to the Chevrolet dealer and check out the Corvette. If I'm really dreaming, I'd peruse the Ferraris and the Lamborghinis. All of these sports cars have powerful, precision-balanced, fine-tuned engines that provide performance plus! Let's say I leased or (since we're dreaming!) bought one. It has almost no miles on it, has a full gas tank, has been oiled and lubricated, and is ready to go. I jump in and—*vroom!*—off I go!

That car might run for a year or even two years, but if I never changed the oil, even that high-performance engine would eventually grind to a halt. It doesn't matter what's under the hood if you don't pay attention to what's in the crankcase. Without fresh oil, even the top-performing car in the world will burn out and be left sitting by the side of the road.

In the same way, there are many Christians who burn out and drop out because they don't know how to maintain fresh oil. I don't care how gifted people are—what they have "under the hood"—they still have to learn how to walk daily under a fresh anointing if they want to keep their gifting fresh. The Holy Spirit imparts gifts to us, but we have to maintain the anointing. It is not automatic. Just as yesterday's movements of the Spirit will not suffice for what God wants to do today, yesterday's anointing will not equip us for the Kingdom work that lies before us today.

Jesus taught us to pray, *"Give us **this day** our daily bread"* (Matt. 6:11). The Israelites in the wilderness gathered every morning only the manna needed for that day because God renewed it every day (see Exod. 16). In the same way, the Holy Spirit renews our anointing on a daily basis—if we let Him. Just as we should not expect or desire to live on yesterday's stale and moldy bread, neither should we expect or desire to function today under yesterday's anointing. Like a high-performance car, we too need fresh oil regularly.

But as I have already said, if we want to receive the anointing, we have to be hungry for it. We have to have a real, deep, desperate, yearning hunger and thirst for the anointing, or we'll never see it. Mild interest or a lukewarm attitude simply won't do. Why should God entrust His anointing to us if we feel as though we could take it or leave it? I did not receive the anointing until I became so tired of things as they were and so desperate for something more that I was ready to pursue it at all costs.

If a man is stranded in the desert, the one thing on his mind is finding water to quench his thirst. Nothing else matters because his survival is at stake. It's the same way with the anointing. If we reach the place where we are ready to do anything or to part with anything in order to get the anointing, that's when we are ready to receive it. God satisfies the hungry and the thirsty (see Isa. 44:3-4). We have to let God fan the hunger in our hearts. I feel so sad for people who are satisfied with the status quo.

Be honest. Are you truly satisfied with the way things are right now in the Church as a whole? Are you satisfied with the level of God's presence and power that you are seeing in your own church? In your own life? Wouldn't you like to see more miracles, more healings, more lost people coming to Christ? If so, then seek fresh oil! Seek it for yourself and for others in your church. Seek it so that the Lord will be glorified in your midst more and more!

# CHAPTER 15
## *Calling the Zadok Priesthood*

I believe that, in the days in which we are now living, God is calling the Zadok priesthood to stand before His people:

> But the priests, the Levites, the sons of Zadok, who kept charge of My sanctuary when the children of Israel went astray from Me, they shall come near Me to minister to Me; and they shall stand before Me to offer to Me the fat and the blood," says the Lord God. "They shall enter My sanctuary, and they shall come near My table to minister to Me, and they shall keep My charge... And they shall teach My people the difference between the holy and the unholy, and cause them to discern between the unclean and the clean (Ezek. 44:15-16,23).

It is a sad state of affairs when even the people of God don't know the difference between the holy and the unholy or the clean and the unclean. Another word for *unholy* is *profane*. I was shocked when I asked the Lord for His definition of *profane*. He said, "The profane is anything people are doing that I did not initiate. It is everything that is empty and worthless and without any eternal value." We must take particular care to make sure that what we're doing is to advance the Kingdom of God and not for our own agendas.

Jesus Christ was the supreme example of this when He said in the Book of John that He did only what He saw His Father doing and said only what He heard His Father saying (see John 5:19; 8:26). That's the secret to maximizing ministry. Don't say anything until you hear what He says. Don't do anything until you see what He is doing.

The real tragedy in the Church today is that we can do things without the Lord's touch and nobody knows the difference. Billy Graham once said that if the Holy Spirit was extracted from the Body of Christ today, few people inside or outside the Church would ever notice any change. For far too long, we have been having church without God, and I believe He's tired of it. I believe He's going to start visiting our churches in a big way, and when He comes, things will be vastly different.

Jesus Christ walked in the anointing, and everywhere He went, people gathered in droves to see Him, to hear Him, to touch Him. Mark records a typical occurrence:

> *And again He entered Capernaum after some days, and it was heard that He was in the house. Immediately many gathered together, so that there was no longer room to receive them, not even near the door. And He preached the word to them* (Mark 2:1-2).

Wouldn't it be something if that verse described your church and mine on a weekly basis? Unfortunately, so many of our churches today have shut Jesus out, often without even being aware of it. And now He stands outside, knocking to be let back in, as with the church in Laodicea: *"Behold, I stand at the door and knock. If anyone hears My voice and opens the door, I will come in to him and dine with him, and he with Me"* (Rev. 3:20). This is why so many Christians don't understand the difference between the holy and the unholy and why so many have lifestyles that are virtually indistinguishable from those of people in the world. Whenever we shut Christ out of our lives and our churches, both lose their distinctiveness. Why should the world flock to the Church if they cannot see that we have anything to offer that they cannot get somewhere else? We need the anointing to restore our distinctiveness in the world.

# CHAPTER 16
## *Divine Empowerment Costs Everything*

Power always comes at a price. In life, there is no such thing as a "free lunch." Something must be given up to gain something else. Sacrifice in the short term is necessary for advantage in the long term. People in business and every other area of life are always asking, "What's the bottom line?" Before committing to anything, they want to know, "How much will this cost?" Counting the cost is a wise move, as long as it doesn't become the sole criterion for our decision or lead us to become cynical. Jesus Himself encouraged us to count the cost of discipleship before committing ourselves to follow Him:

> *Whoever does not bear his cross and come after Me cannot be My disciple. For which of you, intending to build a tower, does not sit down first and count the cost, whether he has enough to finish it—lest, after he has laid the foundation, and is not able to finish, all who see it begin to mock him, saying, "This man began to build and was not able to finish"* (Luke 14:27-30).

So what will it cost to get the anointing? Everything

we have. Not every believer is a serious disciple of Christ, because not every believer chooses to walk in the Spirit. And those who do not walk in the Spirit will not walk in the anointing. Therefore, discipleship and the anointing go hand-in-hand. Just three verses later, Jesus said, *"So likewise, whoever of you does not forsake all that he has cannot be my disciple"* (Luke 14:33).

Don't make the mistake of interpreting this solely in financial or material terms. Following Christ and walking in the anointing may indeed require at times the giving up of some personal conveniences, possessions, or material comforts, but to "forsake all" goes deeper than the material world alone. Jesus is talking here about a heart attitude of holding nothing in this world closer or dearer to us than we hold Him. Everything that we are and have is secondary to following Christ and doing His will. Only such a total sell-out to Jesus qualifies us to carry His anointing. It is in this sense that receiving the anointing will cost us everything.

It will also cost us in the area of suffering. Jesus said that no servant is greater than his master (see John 13:16). How did the world as a whole treat Jesus when He walked in perfect power and perfect love? They hated Him. They spit on Him, beat Him, lashed His back down to the bone, pulled His beard out, nailed Him to a cross naked, and then ridiculed Him as He hung there bleeding and humiliated. If that is the treatment the Master received, what can His servants expect?

The only reason most of us are not suffering or undergoing persecution very much is because we are not walking with Him as closely as we should be. If we want to experience the power of Christ working in us, we need to be willing to experience His suffering as well. Being true disciples of Christ and walking in His anointing means that we must identify with Him in every way, the positive as well as the negative, the pleasant as well as the unpleasant. Paul described the ideal disciple's attitude when he wrote:

> But what things were gain to me, these I have counted loss for Christ. Yet indeed I also count all things loss for the excellence of the knowledge of Christ Jesus my Lord, for whom I have suffered the loss of all things, and count them as rubbish, that I may gain Christ and be found in Him, not having my own righteousness, which is from the law, but that which is through faith in Christ, the righteousness which is from God by faith; that I may know Him and the power of His resurrection, and the fellowship of His sufferings, being conformed to His death, if, by any means, I may attain to the resurrection from the dead. Not that I have already attained, or am already perfected; but I press on, that I may lay hold of that for which Christ Jesus has also laid hold of me. Brethren, I do not count myself to have apprehended; but one thing I do, forgetting those things which are behind and reaching forward to those things which are ahead, I press toward the goal for the prize of the upward call of God in Christ Jesus (Phil. 3:7-14).

Carrying the anointing will, at times, cost us in terms of convenience, time, dignity, reputation, respectability, and persecution. But in the midst of all of these things will come great advancement in the Kingdom of God. And in light of that, all the inconvenience and suffering will fade into insignificance.

Consider the experience of Paul and Silas in Acts chapter 16. Arrested, beaten, and chained to the wall of a prison in Philippi, Paul and Silas could easily have been morose and despondent. Instead, they were heard at midnight, singing and worshiping and praising God! As a result, God rocked the prison with an earthquake, and the shackles fell off of every prisoner in the place! Yet not a single one escaped (see Acts 16:25-34). There is just something magnetic about people anointed by the Holy Spirit who stay true to God, even in the most adverse of circumstances. Not only did all the other inmates stick around to be near Paul and Silas and their message, but also the warden of the prison and his entire family came to Christ that night. No matter the situation, the anointing of the Lord can empower and enable us to present a faithful and winsome witness that can lead to lives being forever changed in Christ. Are you hungry for that kind of spiritual power and the influence to see people's lives changed?

# CHAPTER 17
## *How to Get Divine Empowerment*

I hope that by now you are so hungry for the anointing that you can almost taste it! I hope you are squirming in your chair saying, "OK, Bobby, OK! You've convinced me! I need the empowering and enabling anointing, and I want the anointing! Now how do I get it?" Remember, there is no "magic formula" for the anointing, and it is not reserved for an elite group of Christian "superstars." Any Christian who is hungry enough to make the necessary preparations of heart, mind, will, and spirit can receive the anointing.

### FOUR INSIGHTS FOR EMPOWERMENT

Let's talk about four steps for receiving the anointing. The first two will be a review because I've already talked about them in this book. They are so important, however, and so indispensable, that they bear repeating.

First, we must become discontent with any dry, dead, and empty form of religion and get desperate for a fresh move of God in our lives. We must have a deep hunger and longing for more of the presence of God. We must cry out for God like a man in the desert cries out for water. *"I stretch forth my hands unto thee: my soul thirsteth after thee, as a thirsty land"* (Ps. 143:6 KJV). When we get desperate and begin to seek for the Lord with all of our hearts, then He will be found. God is looking for those who are longing for His anointing. God wants to pour His Spirit out upon us like a flood. If we are longing for the Lord, deeply desiring Him, and truly seeking Him, we are on the right road to receiving the anointing. *"Then you will call upon Me and go and pray to Me, and I will listen to you. And you will seek Me and find Me, when you search for Me with all your heart"* (Jer. 29:12-13). Are we hungry? Are we desperate? Do we thirst after the Lord and His anointing like a parched land thirsts for water? I hope so. That's the first step.

The second step to receiving the anointing is to be clean and pure. Ecclesiastes 9:8 says, *"Let your garments be always white; and let your head lack no oil."* To be vessels that the Lord would delight to use, we must be clean. To this end, we must regularly ask God to have the Holy Spirit search our hearts and convict us of any hidden or known sins. After the Holy Spirit has searched our hearts and convicted us of sin, we must sincerely confess our sins and repent. *"If we confess our sins, He is faithful and just to forgive us our sins and to cleanse us from all unrighteousness"* (1 John 1:9). Let's put our sins under the precious cleansing blood of Jesus. When we do, this is His promise: *"Though your sins are like scarlet, they shall be as white as snow; though they are red like crimson, they shall be as wool"* (Isa. 1:18b). It is easy to overlook or to give short shrift to the process of confession and repentance of sin. Besides the fact that it is often an unpleasant process that we would rather ignore, we are so eager to pursue the "good stuff" of the anointing that we short circuit the process when we do not deal adequately with the sin and uncleanliness in our lives. We must not pass over this step lightly!

The third step to receiving the anointing is to ask the Heavenly Father to anoint us and fill us afresh with the power of the Holy Spirit. Often we do not have because we have not asked.

*So I say to you, ask, and it will be given to you; seek and you will find; knock, and it will be opened to you. For everyone who asks receives, and he who seeks finds, and to him who knocks it will be opened* (Luke 11:9-10).

In an earlier chapter, I shared with you how I became so discouraged at the lack of true spiritual power in my ministry that I was ready to quit. I knew there had to be more, so I began a personal quest for the Holy Spirit. It was quite a journey. First, I went to my best friend, a Bible teacher whom I loved and respected, and I asked him if he knew how to get filled with the Holy Spirit. He said he thought it came by the laying on of hands. So he laid hands on me and prayed for me, but all it did was mess up my hair. That wasn't the way.

My next stop in my quest was going to seminary. Seeking counsel from one of the theological experts at the school, I cited the verses in Mark 16 about the signs that would follow those who believed. He patted me on the head, like a puppy, and told me those verses weren't supposed to be in the Bible—that they were a later addition. Then he advised me to leave those verses alone or else they would "mess up" my ministry. He was right. My ministry needed to be messed up! I didn't find the answer to my quest at seminary.

Then I thought I would try the Pentecostal church. After all, Pentecostals had the Holy Spirit, didn't they? A Southern Baptist preacher going to the Pentecostals—I was desperate! I had never been in a service like that before. Everybody was whooping and hollering and singing and shouting. It was pretty vibrant in that place. The preacher really preached up a storm and afterward, when he was standing at the front, I went down to him and said, "My name's Bobby Conner. I'm a southern Baptist pastor. I've come because I'm looking for the Holy Ghost." The place went nuts! The pastor fell over, leaving me standing there. People in the congregation jumped up and started running around the church whooping and hollering and dancing. They threw me down over the prayer altar. I mean, they were all over me. I finally crawled under the piano bench and asked them to leave me alone so I could pray!

I said, "Lord?"

He said, "Get up, Bobby. This is not Me." So I got up and left, but I still didn't have my answer.

I had gone to my best friend, I had gone to seminary, and I had gone to the Pentecostal church looking for the Holy Spirit. I had been on this quest for weeks. While driving home, I prayed, "Lord Jesus, what do I do?"

He said, "I've been waiting for this." He brought to my mind Luke 11:13, where Jesus said, *"If you then, being evil, know how to give good gifts to your children, how much more will your heavenly Father give the Holy Spirit to those who ask Him!"*

So I asked Him, and the Holy Spirit fell on me. What happened? I began to develop a wonderful appreciation for the Word of God. It was like a geyser, like an overflow of life. God's Word was no longer just something I studied to prepare a sermon. It was an absolute love letter from God feeding my life. One thing I have learned is, we can't have the power of God if we're afraid of the Spirit of God. If we want God to anoint us, we can simply ask Him.

The fourth step to receiving and walking in the anointing is starting to confess what God's Word has to say about us— instead of confessing how we feel. Let's confess confidence in Christ's ability in us and learn to speak not what we feel, but what God's Word teaches. If we see ourselves as weak and unworthy and not fit for service, that is exactly how the enemy will see us, too. What we think about ourselves determines how we will act. Our beliefs always affect our behavior. As Proverbs 23:7 says, *"For as he thinks in his heart, so is he..."* We must fill our hearts with faith, not fear. And faith comes by hearing the Word of God. *"So then faith comes by hearing, and hearing by the word of God"* (Rom. 10:17).

One of the most encouraging words the Lord has ever spoken to me was when He said, "Now people are getting power hungry for all the right reasons." This addresses the question of why we want the anointing. Is it so that people will look at us and say, "Oh, he (or she) has the anointing"? No. We want the anointing so that people will look at us, but see Christ! That's what we have to do to walk in true anointing—put Christ on display in our lives. Paul said, *"But we all, with unveiled face, beholding as in a mirror the glory of the Lord, are being transformed into the same image from glory to glory, just as by the Spirit of the Lord"* (2 Cor. 3:18). We are being transformed from glory to glory. The New International Version says we're changed *"into His likeness with ever-increasing glory."*

Isn't that what you want? Don't you want the presence and power of Christ in your life so completely that when people look at you, they will not see you, but will see Christ in you? That's what the anointing is all about.

# CHAPTER 18
## *Abiding in Authority and Empowerment*

Receiving the anointing is one thing; abiding or walking in it is another. Discontent with empty religion and the status quo may have made you desperately hungry for a fresh move of God in your life. In your desperation, you have examined your heart—and asked God to examine it—and you have dealt with any sin or other hindrance found there through confession and repentance. Now, in the assurance of the purifying and cleansing work of the Spirit in your heart, you have asked God to anoint you and fill you afresh with the Holy Spirit's power. You have begun confessing what God's Word says about you with confidence in Christ's ability in you. And God has given you His anointing—a fresh touch of His Spirit. Now what? How do you maintain this fresh, wonderful anointing that you have received? How do you walk in it day by day and keep it fresh and new and powerful in your life?

Above all, we must keep in mind that just as we did not receive the anointing through our own wisdom or power, we also cannot maintain it or walk in it in our own strength alone. Abiding in the anointing is a lifestyle of humility—of complete and utter dependence on God. Nevertheless, there are several attitudes or character traits that will help us stay in the necessary spiritual posture to walk consistently in the anointing. We will look at four: accessibility, teachability, restorability, and availability.

## ACCESSIBILITY

Those who would walk in the anointing must be accessible, not only to God, but also to other people. If there is one thing the Gospels make clear about Jesus Christ, it is that He was accessible. Jesus was on a vitally important mission from His Father—to proclaim the coming of the Kingdom of God and to die for the sins of humanity so that we could enter it—and He never allowed Himself to be diverted from that mission. At the same time, He was never too busy to touch, heal, and minister to anyone who came to Him.

Most of us have probably known leaders, even Christian leaders, who have become so big and so important (or self-important, as is usually the case) that they are beyond the reach of the "ordinary" people. That's the "superstar syndrome," and it has no place in Christian discipleship. God prefers to use ordinary folks like you and me. Walking in the anointing means remembering that we are ordinary people who are carrying an extraordinary anointing from an extraordinary God in order to carry out extraordinary things.

Some people, once they receive any degree of the anointing, suddenly become inaccessible. They get too close to the anointing and begin glorying in the anointing instead of in the One who gives the anointing. Because of this, they shut themselves off from the "less fortunate" who have not been "touched" as they have. One of the fastest ways to shut down the anointing is to allow ourselves to get too big for our britches. If we are full of ourselves, we cannot be full of the anointing. Remember, this is not about us, but about Him—it is all about Him!

Even Jesus never claimed to do anything on His own. He said and did only what He saw His Father saying and doing (see John 5:19; 8:26). And He was always accessible. He loved and welcomed children near Him, and He blessed them. On at least one occasion, He rebuked His disciples for trying to send them away (see Matt. 19:13-15). Jesus willingly and openly associated with tax collectors and sinners (see Matt. 9:10-13), the unclean, the castoffs, the dregs of society—the very people who needed Him most and who were ignored by everybody else. Although ridiculed and criticized by the self-righteous in society, Jesus was not afraid of losing His reputation. He had willingly *"made Himself of no reputation"* in order to win our salvation. And as His disciples, we are to do the same. Paul put it this way:

*Let this mind be in you which was also in Christ Jesus, who, being in the form of God, did not consider it robbery to be equal with God, but made Himself of no reputation, taking the form of a bondservant, and coming in the likeness of men. And being found in appearance as a man, He humbled Himself and became obedient to the point of death, even the death of the cross* (Phil. 2:5-8).

Jesus could not have done this without making Himself accessible. And we cannot walk consistently in the anointing without being accessible, too. We cannot be so protective of our dignity and reputation or so fearful of being vulnerable that we close ourselves off from others.

One day, while passing through Jericho, Jesus stopped at the foot of a large sycamore tree. He looked up at the small man who was gazing down at him from its branches and said, *"Zacchaeus, make haste and come down, for today I must stay at your house"* (Luke 19:5b). Zacchaeus was thrilled and hurried down, but the crowd around Jesus was scandalized because Zacchaeus was a crooked collaborator. As a tax collector for the Romans, he routinely cheated his own people to line his own pockets. It was little wonder that they hated him. And many of the upright citizens of Jericho were offended when Jesus chose to stay with such a man. Zacchaeus represents all of those people who live a shady life and are hungry for God, but don't want anybody to know they're hungry. Being a short man, Zacchaeus climbed the sycamore tree so he could see Jesus, but he didn't want anyone to see the hunger in his heart. Not, at least, until Jesus called him. Then he didn't care. He scrambled out of that tree and received Jesus with joy, not only into his home, but also into his heart. Look what happened:

*Then Zacchaeus stood and said to the Lord, "Look, Lord, I give half of my goods to the poor; and if I have taken anything from anyone by false accusation, I restore fourfold." And Jesus said to him, "Today salvation has come to this house, because he also is a son of Abraham; for the Son of Man has come to seek and to save that which was lost"* (Luke 19:8-10).

Zacchaeus' life and eternal destiny were transformed forever. But it never would have happened if Jesus had not made Himself accessible. Accessibility was a key to Jesus' mission, which was *"to seek and to save that which was lost."* He could not do that without going to where the lost could be found. He could not do it without being accessible. The more accessible we are, the more God will be able to use us to touch and transform the lives of others. If we want to walk in the anointing, we need to be accessible.

## TEACHABILITY

Along with accessibility comes teachability, a teachable spirit. Just because you carry the anointing does not mean you have nothing else to learn. On the contrary, a disciple is always learning—that's the meaning of the word *disciple*. Many people today, including many in the Church, seem to display an attitude that there is nothing anyone can teach them, especially those of an earlier and older generation. Unless it's brand new and completely fresh, they don't want it. To be sure, God is always doing something new, and we always need a fresh anointing, but the anointing and the new things that God does are always about His eternal Kingdom and the timeless gospel of Christ—things that never change. So we need both the old and the new. And we need humble spirits that are willing to learn from those who can teach us.

In my first pastorate, many years ago, I was a young, strapping, wild sort of guy, strong as an ox. One of my church members was the old Mr. Clayton. Skinny, wiry, and in his early seventies, Mr. Clayton had bodily strength that belied his age and size. I discovered this one day when we went to cut down some trees on a plot of land where we were going to construct a new church building. The trees needed to go in order to give a survey team access to take measurements.

Mr. Clayton got his long-handled ax out of his car and went to work. He'd go whack, and that ax cut deep into that tree with every stroke. In minutes, the tree was down and he moved on to another. After felling several trees, he stopped and wiped his brow with a handkerchief. I'd been watching all of this and, knowing I was strong, I said to him, "Mr. Clayton, give me that ax. Let me do some of the work."

He looked at me and asked, "Do you know how to use an ax?"

"Sure, "I replied. "I know how to use an ax." I walked over to a sapling, a little tree no more than two or three inches in diameter, and I was going to show Mr. Clayton how well I could use that ax. Putting my back into it, I took a mighty swing—and missed. I gnarled up the ax handle a little, and

Mr. Clayton gave me a look that said, "Boy you don't know nothing about axes do you?" I took one more swing and nearly broke the ax handle. That's when he took it back from me and went back to work. I was strong, but strength alone wasn't enough. I also needed knowledge. There was a lot I needed to learn from Mr. Clayton.

When I was in high school, I used to make some extra money loading watermelons. Some of my friends and I, all of us football players, would go to the farmers' market where the farmers brought their watermelons in on trucks, and we were paid to transfer the melons from the trucks to train boxcars. It was a good physical workout for us and helped us stay in shape, and we got paid besides, so what wasn't to like?

Those were the days when farmers grew really large watermelons, much larger than what you usually find today. One of us would pick up a melon, carry it over and hand it to the next guy in line, who would carry it to the next guy, and so on until the last one loaded it onto the boxcar. This went on for a little while, and the whole time an old guy sat watching us from under a tree next to the courthouse. He was as skinny as a lizard. After watching us for a while, he walked over, spat out a big brown wad of chewing tobacco on the ground and said, "You boys don't know nothing about loading melons do ya?"

"What do you mean?" I asked. "Sure we can load watermelons."

"Not very well."

"I suppose you can load them, with those scrawny little arms of yours?"

He said, "I can load them better than you can."

I doubted it, but said, "OK, show us."

And he did. He was right; he could load them better than

we could! The secret he taught us was in how to let go of the melon. We had been doing it wrong. I would pick up a melon, give it to Randy, who would give it to Thomas, and so on. That's not how you load watermelons. The way you load watermelons is by picking them up and tossing them. Instead of carrying it, you just pitch it to the next person in line. Then it becomes easy. From the momentum of my toss, Randy would catch it and pitch it to Thomas in one smooth motion. It's all in the knowing how. And sometimes we learn from the most unlikely teachers.

I believe many of us struggle with our burdens the way Randy, Thomas, and I struggled with those watermelons. By the time that skinny, old man was finished with us, we could load watermelons all day long and never get a sore back. He was like the Holy Spirit, teaching us a better way. A teachable spirit requires humility. And instead of carrying our burdens, we are supposed to cast them on the Lord. As Peter counseled us, *"Therefore humble yourselves under the mighty hand of God, that He may exalt you in due time, casting all your care upon Him, for He cares for you"* (1 Pet. 5:6-7). We have to learn to let go of our burdens and let the momentum carry them away.

Without a teachable spirit, we will never be able to sustain the anointing because it comes from the Spirit of God, who is our teacher. Jesus said, *"But the Helper, the Holy Spirit, whom the Father will send in My name, He will teach you all things, and bring to your remembrance all things that I said to you"* (John 14:26). If we are teachable, the Lord will teach us. We just can't be surprised at who He sends to do the job!

## RESTORABILITY

Another vital mindset for walking in the anointing is the attitude of restorability. Because we are sinners saved by grace, we are not perfect. We will make mistakes. At times, we will yield to temptation. We will slip into sin. Restorability means understanding that, while some failure along the way is inevitable, failure is never final. There is always a way back. Just as any believer who is hungry and desperate for the anointing can receive it, any believer who has fallen or who has stepped out from under the anointing can be restored. God is able and willing to bring restoration. He does not will that any of His children be isolated from Him or relegate themselves to lives of defeat and frustration. The restoration of the anointing can be illustrated by an event in the life of the Old Testament prophet Elisha.

*And the sons of the prophets said to Elisha, "See now, the place where we dwell with you is too small for us. Please, let us go to the Jordan, and let every man take a beam from there, and let us make there a place where we may dwell." So he answered, "Go." Then one said, "Please consent to go with your servants." And he answered, "I will go." So he went with them. And when they came to the Jordan, they cut down trees. But as one was cutting down a tree, the iron ax head fell into the water; and he cried out and said, "Alas, master! For it was borrowed." So the man of God said, "Where did it fall?" And he showed him the place. So he cut off a stick, and threw it in there; and he made the iron float. Therefore he said, "Pick it up for yourself." So he reached out his hand and took it* (2 Kings 6:1-7).*

The "sons of the prophets" were prophets in training, and Elisha was their teacher. They decided they needed bigger lodgings, so they asked Elisha for permission to cut down trees at the Jordan River to use in building new quarters. When Elisha granted permission, one of the students asked him to accompany them, and Elisha consented. Like Jesus several centuries later, Elisha was accessible. The leader went with his students. He did not abandon them to their own devices. The prophetic is more caught than taught. If people get around it long enough, it just kind of rubs off on them. The stage was being set for a miracle. One of these prophets in training was cutting down a tree next to the river, and the ax head fell off into the water. Maybe he got distracted or didn't know how to use an ax (where's Mr. Clayton when you need him!), but for some reason unknown to us, the ax head fell off the handle. There wasn't much he could do with only an ax handle. He could have played games. He could have said, "I'm going to continue to hit and act like I'm working. Maybe nobody will notice that my tree is not falling." That represents empty religious activity and useless busyness, which is where much of the Church is today. They are swinging and sweating, but no trees are falling—and they don't realize that their ax has lost its head. Why? They have lost the anointing. To his everlasting credit, however, this young prophet-to-be was not content to go through the motions. What about you? Aren't you tired of going through the motions? Aren't you tired of a lot of swinging and sweating and striving and keeping up a good appearance?

Look what this young man did. He called to Elisha, *"Alas, master, for it was borrowed."* Whenever we forget that the gift is from God and start acting like it belongs to us, we can lose it. Any anointing we receive comes from God, not from our own initiative. As James says, *"Every good gift and every perfect gift is from above, and comes down from the Father of lights, with whom there is no variation or shadow of turning"* (James 1:17). I love Elisha's response: *"Where did it fall?"* Where did we lose the anointing? Where did we become separated from the power of God? Perhaps it was when we began to compromise with political agendas. Maybe we lost it because of the fear of people, becoming more concerned about what others think than about what God wants. Or perhaps the anointing departed when sin entered our hearts and pushed it out. Whatever the reason, we have to come to grips with where it fell.

When Elisha asked, *"Where did it fall?"* the man showed him the spot. He knew exactly where he had been standing when the ax head fell off. We can't look in all the wrong places for restoration of what we need. We have to know where we lost it and return to that place to find it again. And we have to be honest with ourselves and with God. If we want to experience a restoration of power and the anointing, we need to get brazenly and boldly honest. The man could have tried to cover himself and say, "I don't know where I lost it." And he would have missed his blessing. Instead, he was honest and experienced a miracle.

Elisha took a stick and cast it into the water over the spot where the ax head had disappeared. Then, the iron ax head floated. I believe that stick represents the cross of Christ. Through the cross, Christ restores to us everything that we've lost. Imagine the young prophet's amazement when Elisha threw the stick in and the water started gurgling and bubbling and then the ax head suddenly bobbed to the surface! That which he feared was lost forever was restored, and he regained his ability to perform the job that God had assigned to him.

Notice, too, that Elisha did not retrieve the ax head and put it back on the handle. Instead, he instructed his student, *"Pick it up for yourself."* I think this is a very important point. This is the same thing we're going to have to do in our churches. The prophets are going to have to do what God calls them to do. They're going to have to find out where the power of God was lost, and then they're going to have to say, "Pick it up for yourself." Personally, I believe that when this student picked up the ax head and put it back on the handle—when his power and anointing were restored—he felled more trees than all the rest of them. I think he made every stroke count. He had been restored. He had a second chance, and I believe he made the most of it.

Wisdom is always better than might. If we want restoration, if we want to walk in the anointing consistently, we have to believe in miracles. We have to believe that God can restore to the Church what has been lost due to sin, ignorance, compromise, and unbelief.

Here's another interesting point: The ax head fell into the Jordan River. In the Bible, the Jordan River often represents that which stands in the way of the people of God receiving what He has promised. One particular feature of the Jordan River is that it overflows its banks at harvest time. Yet, in the Book of Joshua, that was the time of year when God commanded Joshua and the Israelites to cross the Jordan into Canaan, the Promised Land. He instructed them to cross at the precise time when the river was at its widest and deepest point and when its current was at its fastest. Have you ever noticed how God often directs us to advance at the most inopportune times? We'd rather wait until after harvest time, when the water goes down, but God prefers that we advance under the most adverse situations. He does this so that He can receive the glory. He wants to leave no doubt in anyone's mind as to who did it. God is glorified when the world sees us do something beyond our power to do, something that only God can do.

When the Israelites got ready to cross the Jordan, the priests bearing the ark of the covenant led the way. As the priests stepped into the waters of the river, the water rolled up all the way back to the city of Adam, and the children of Israel went across on dry ground (see Josh. 3:14-17). No matter what our personal Jordan may be, whatever stands between us and what God has promised us, God can move it out of the way. He can make a way when it seems like there is no way. We have to believe that we can be restored. We have to believe that we can recover what the enemy stole from us. God wants to restore it. He wants to restore us when we need restoring.

Aren't you tired of just swinging the handle with no head? One of the saddest verses in the Bible is Jeremiah 8:20: *"The harvest is past, the summer is ended, and we are not saved!"* You don't want that to happen. You don't want to miss the day of your visitation. For this reason, God is asking you the question, "Where did it fall?" Where did you really begin to wane in your walk with the Lord? And why? If you want a change, you have to come clean and be brutally honest. It won't do to simply shrug your shoulders and say, "I don't know." If you ask the Lord, He'll show you where you departed from Him. As James says:

> *If any of you lacks wisdom, let him ask of God, who gives to all liberally and without reproach, and it will be given to him. But let him ask in faith, with no doubting, for he who doubts is like a wave of the sea driven and tossed by the wind. For let not that man suppose that he will receive anything from the Lord; he is a double-minded man, unstable in all his ways* (James 1:5-8).

Remember, failure is never final. Instead, we must believe in our restorability and in His power and willingness to restore. And He is willing. There is always a way back into the grace and favor and anointing and power of the Lord. He's always calling us back.

## AVAILABILITY

If walking in the anointing means being accessible to people, it also means being available to God. This calls for an attitude of humility, recognizing how utterly dependent we are upon Him. People who feel self-sufficient in their own strength do not make themselves available to God because they don't see the need. God calls the ordinary, the outcasts, the desperate, and the destitute. He calls the very people who know that without Him they don't have a prayer. God calls the "Jephthahs" of the world.

On the Day of Atonement a few years ago, I had a vision in which the Lord Jesus appeared in the doorway. A bright light shone from behind Him, and He said, "Bobby, I want you to meet your brother." My only brother was killed by lightning on May 29, 1979, so I thought this word from the Lord was quite strange. Then He gestured with His hand, as if introducing someone, and a figure stepped through the doorway.

The Lord said, "Meet your brother, Jephthah."

In the Bible, Jephthah was an outcast, the son of a harlot, and he was driven off by his half-brothers, the legitimate sons of their common father. He also had a reputation as a "mighty man of valor." His story is recorded in the 11th chapter of the Book of Judges. Denied his inheritance because of his parentage, Jephthah knew what it was to suffer bitter, horrible betrayal. Years later, however, when those same brothers stood in need of a valiant champion, they turned to Jephthah.

When the Ammonites invaded and made trouble for Israel, Jephthah's people, the Gileadites, brought him back from exile and asked him to lead them. After understandably questioning why they had come to him (since they had thrown him out), and after receiving assurances from them that he would not be cast out again, Jephthah stepped up as the leader and the liberator of the children of Israel. He overcame bitter betrayal—something that God is going to do again. Today there are many Jephthahs outside the door who have been cast out by self-righteous brothers. And God's going to bring them back in.

The first thing Jephthah did was to talk to the enemy. He tried to negotiate with words, and they wouldn't negotiate. Then he said, "How dare you come and violate my land?" Very quickly he re-associated himself with his brothers. He called it his land, his inheritance. The very land that he had been kicked off of and the very inheritance that he had been denied were his again. When the opportunity for restoration came, Jephthah made himself available.

God's going to bring in the outcasts. Some of God's very best leaders are not in the Church right now; they've been cast out. But God is in the process of calling them back in, and we'd better get ready for them. Some of the strongest leaders will be people we've never heard of. They're going to come to the front so quickly that our heads are going to spin.

Who knows? Maybe you will be one of them! Don't forget that God can anoint anyone and use anyone for any purpose He desires. If it serves His purpose, He can exalt any one of us higher than we could ever imagine, or He can use us in places where only a few will ever know who we are. The place of service and level of notoriety are not important; being available to the Lord for whatever purpose He chooses is what matters.

One of the things we need to understand is that, when we get the Holy Spirit, He can give us any gift He wills. I've heard people say that we shouldn't seek after spiritual things, yet the Bible tells us specifically to desire spiritual gifts (see 1 Cor. 14:1). We should seek after them and pursue them. Some people even say that we shouldn't talk about the supernatural. However, hundreds of verses in the Bible talk about the supernatural, and the Bible clearly tells us to expect miracles.

As disciples who want to walk consistently in the anointing, we need to make ourselves available for the Holy Spirit to give us any gift He wishes. I've seen some people who hold out for a specific gift. They are unwilling to work or serve unless it is in the specific area that they desire. With that attitude, they will never walk in the anointing and never know the joy and satisfaction of being used of God. For my part, I'll take any gift the Spirit wants to give me, in any way He chooses to give it! I want to be available. The Bible says that the Spirit imparts gifts as He chooses (see 1 Cor. 12:11). We have the potential to receive any gift, but the choice of gift is His, not ours. Our part is to make ourselves available.

With the Holy Spirit living inside us, any gift that He has is available to us. If we are drawn to a particular gift, which we see operating in someone else, we can ask the Lord for it. Then we must position our hearts, allowing for His sovereignty and ultimate will. I believe that, in many cases, He will give it to us if we are willing to do what the person (in whom we saw it operating) did to get it. Many times we look at somebody who is walking under an anointing or walking under a real grace of God, and we think, *Oh man, I want that.* The question is, are we willing to do what that person did to get it?

The anointing is for us if we have the passion and the hunger for it. It is a sovereign work of God in our lives to prepare us for service and ministry. Philippians 2:13 says, *"For it is God who works in you both to will and to do for His good pleasure."* God Himself works in us to give us the will to work for Him. We don't just wake up one day and decide on our own to do something great for God. No, it is God who wills it and who works it in us. He is the one who qualifies and not us. The Holy Spirit comes inside of us and anoints us to do any task that God assigns to us. We have to quit feeling like we're inferior for the task. Instead, we need to start saying, "I am well able." We need to agree with Paul, who said, *"I can do all things through Christ who strengthens me"* (Phil. 4:13).

Affirming our ability, as God makes us able, puts us in company with Caleb. Caleb and Joshua alone—out of the entire generation of Israelites who left Egypt—lived to enter the Promised Land because they remained faithful to believe in and act upon God's promises. When finally, at the age of eighty-five, Caleb was ready to claim the inheritance for which he had waited so long, he said, *"As yet I am as strong this day as on the day that Moses sent me; just as my strength was then, so now is my strength for war, both for going out and for coming in"* (Josh. 14:11).

Caleb's name means "salty old dog, tenacious one." He was the one who wouldn't let go. Let's be like Caleb, refusing to let go of our dreams, no matter what. Whatever God has promised us, let us hang on to those promises. If we remain faithful, tenacious, and available, He will bring to pass everything He has promised us. Though it may seem long in coming, we must not cast it away.

It says in Hebrews:

> *Therefore do not cast away your confidence, which has great reward. For you have need of endurance, so that after you have done the will of God, you may receive the promise: "For yet a little while, and He who is coming will come and will not tarry. Now the just shall live by faith; but if anyone draws back, My soul has no pleasure in him"* (Heb. 10:35-38).

*"Don't cast away your confidence, which has great reward."* One translation says, *"Don't fling away from you this lively hope."* In other words, we must not give up or give in to discouragement if things do not happen in the timing or manner that we prefer. Rather, we must let God choose

the manner and the timing. His will is always best. Many people think they're going to get a prophetic anointing and—snap—their breakthrough will come just that fast. Most of the time, it doesn't work that way. God promised the children of Israel an inheritance in a land flowing with milk and honey. Then He led them out of Egypt into the desert. Did God lie? No, the Bible says He led them into the desert to test their hearts (see Deut. 8:2). And most of them failed the test. They complained to Moses, "Why did you bring us out here to die? It would have been better if we had stayed in Egypt" (see Exod. 16:3).

Learn from the Israelites and don't long for Egypt. Don't look back to what once was. Your future lies ahead of you, and your destiny awaits. Advance into it with confidence. The only direction is forward. Be accessible. Be teachable. Be restorable. Be available. Step into the anointing that God has for you, and walk in it with Him! It's what you were born to do! You are empowered for victory!

# CHAPTER 19
## *The Type of Leaders God Uses*

Who are these coming leaders? Are they special people with amazing giftings and anointings? Not necessarily. This is one of the deceptions we must erase—that God only uses special people. Nothing could be more distant from biblical truth (see 1 Cor. 1:26). These coming leaders are "whosoever will"—a phrase that Jesus used often to indicate our choice in the matter (see Matt. 7:24; 10:32-33; 16:25; 20:26-27; Mark 3:35; 8:34-35 KJV). In other words, each one of us could be one of them.

We must remember that the Lord is looking for a people whose hearts are right with Him so that He can fully support all that they are doing (see 2 Chron. 16:9). For this reason, the Spirit of Truth is raising up leaders with integrity and character who will teach us the vast difference between what is pure and what is profane (see Ezek. 44:23). We must raise the standard! These are unusual days of destiny, and we must arise to the challenge. God is looking for the ordinary saints whose hearts are passionately burning for the establishing of the King in His Kingdom.

Consequently, it is crucial that we walk in uprightness if we are to ascend the hill of the Lord (see Ps. 24:4-6). As we embrace accountability, we can be trusted with more true spiritual authority. Christ Jesus informed us that if we are faithful over little, we will become rulers over much more (see Matt. 25:21). On the other hand, if we fail to handle small things correctly, even the small things are in danger of being removed.

## A PROPHETIC PROMISE FROM THE LORD

In a vivid prophetic experience, the Spirit of the Lord spoke these encouraging words to me: "Accept no imitations! Expect no limitations! Embrace infinite possibilities!" As we aspire to make these three directives a living reality in our lives, we will see the Church launched into a much higher level of God's power.

### Accept No Imitations

*Artificial, counterfeit, synthetic*—these are a few of the words that help us to better understand the meaning of the word *imitation*. I once asked a bank president, "How do your tellers detect a counterfeit bill?"

His answer was profound. "The best way to expose phony money is to be so accustomed to handling the real thing that when you touch a fake, something within you instantly sets off a warning."

This is what the Body of Christ must have—true intimacy with Jesus that instantly reveals any imitation. We must become so accustomed to His voice that the enticing stranger's voice does not move us. If we are the sheep of His fold, we must come to know and follow our Shepherd's voice. The world's siren song attempts to lure believers from the heavenly sound that resonates in our spirits. We cannot continue to spend our lives on that which is false and worthless. All wood, hay, and stubble must be removed (see 1 Cor. 3:12-15).

We see the call for apostolic living in the message of the Book of Jude. It sounds as a piercing bell to the end-time Church age. The warning is all too clear: If we do not return to the acts of the apostles, we will continue to see the actions of the apostates. It is imperative that we become contenders and defenders of the faith. We are urged to *"contend for the faith that was once for all entrusted to the saints"* (Jude 3 NIV).

### Expect No Limitations

If we will refuse imitations and walk in unadulterated relationship with Christ, then we can expect no limitations. Jesus said in Matthew 9:29, *"According to your faith be it unto you"* (KJV). If we will expect more, God will release more. It is time now to begin to embrace the formation of character within us that will release God's infinite possibilities.

The world is waiting to see a true display of God's power. It is not enough for us to just talk about God's awesome actions; we must display them. As we discover in First Corinthians 4:20, it was never God's plan to establish His Kingdom with mere words, but with power. Similarly, in Hebrews 11:1, we find that active faith produces two much-needed elements: substance and evidence. The Spirit of God will release upon us living proof of God's power if we are willing to yield ourselves completely to Him. As Paul stated in First Corinthians 2:1-5, he did not depend upon enticing words of human wisdom, but rather upon the power of God's Spirit to convince people of their need of Christ. *"'Not by might nor by power, but by My Spirit,' says the Lord of hosts"* (Zech. 4:6).

My heart is encouraged by these faith-building statements from a precious and powerful woman who achieved much for the Kingdom in her day—Kathryn Kuhlman:

- The only limit to the power of God lies within the individual.

- It is when active faith dares to believe God to the point of action that something has to happen.

Sister Kuhlman walked in an awesome anointing for the supernatural because she was willing to fully follow the Lord. Only as we lay down our ways and yielded to His way will we truly see the infinite power of God manifested in our lives.

### Embrace Infinite Possibilities

In order to embrace someone, we must first draw near, reach forth our hands, take hold of Him, and bring Him near to our hearts. A true embrace is heart-to-heart; there is no such thing as a distant embrace. We cannot embrace this coming move of God from a distance. He is calling each of us to draw nearer to Him, leaving behind our complacent attitudes. Now is the time to come aside, to know His heart. In Psalm 46:10, we are instructed to be still and know that He is the Lord. It is only as we behold His face that we are truly changed into His divine image (see 2 Cor. 3:18). To begin this process, the first step is to meditate upon His promises.

Once, the Lord spoke these encouraging words to me: "If I can find a people without mixture, I will pour out My power without measure." Along these lines, Revelation 3:20-22 tells us that a group of overcomers will walk in true Kingdom power. This causes three questions to arise in my heart: *If not you, who? If not here, where? If not now, when?* I cannot emphasize these questions enough:

**Why not you?** Yes, you, the one reading this chapter, feeling inadequate and unqualified. Read the Word and cry out to God for more faith. Never forget that you are special to God; He only created one in the entire world like you, and He desires to use you in a uniquely divine manner.

**Why not here?** Why not in your life, your family's life,

your workplace, and your city? Many believe that, if they could only change their environment, then God could use them. However, you must remember where John was when he had his greatest encounter with the Living Christ—on a rock island serving as a prisoner (see Rev. 1:9).

**Why not now?** Ask God to give you grace to totally abandon yourself to Him and His glorious calling on your life. You will find Him when you search for Him with all your heart (see Jer. 29:12).

Genesis 18:14 poses the question, *"Is anything too hard for the Lord?"* The prophet Jeremiah clearly answers: *"Ah, Sovereign Lord, you have made the heaven and the earth by your great power and outstretched arm. Nothing is too hard for you"* (Jer. 32:17 NIV). The cry of our souls must be— "God, nothing is impossible with You!"

Let's pray for big faith that moves God's hand. Now is the time to think big. God can do anything. It is time to expect more, believe for more, and ask for more. Paul the apostle reminded us, God *"is able to do exceeding abundantly above all we ask or think, according to the power that works in us"* (Eph. 3:20). I love what Smith Wigglesworth said: "There are boundless possibilities for us, if we dare to act in God and dare to believe."

## TRANSITION PRODUCES TRANSFORMATION

Presently, these emerging leaders are in a season of sifting and pruning—the refiner's fire is forging their character to carry this unique anointing. Many feel a sense of disorientation at this time; this is the result of spinning on the "Potter's wheel." Seasons of change never feel comfortable.

However, we can be assured the Master Potter Himself is about to touch the soft pliable clay, and soon we will bear His image. We are in a time of transition that will produce transformation. Our responsibility is to remain soft and moist—yielded upon the Master's wheel. If we attempt to mold ourselves or if we allow ourselves to become dry and brittle, we must be broken and remolded. It is imperative that we stay soft and surrendered before the Lord.

## CHARACTER—NOT JUST GIFTING

The refiner's fire is absolutely purifying these leaders so that the anointing will not be lost or the wineskins damaged or destroyed for lack of character. A steward is required to be faithful. Unfortunately, we've seen many tragic examples of great giftings in people who lacked the character needed to steward them appropriately. God will impart the divine nature and holy character established in the Spirit of the Lord. These emerging leaders and counselors will not judge by what their eyes see or what their ears hear, but in true righteousness they will make decisions resulting in equity and justice.

It is crucial for the Church to begin walking in true apostolic authority. If we are going to be trusted with a higher level of authority, it is essential for us to walk in integrity and uprightness (see Heb. 12:14). The instructions are extremely clear in First Peter 1:13-16: *"Gird up the lions of your mind, be sober..."* God is serious about His children living upright lives. Verse 16 goes on to say: *"Because it is written, 'Be holy, for I am holy.'"* Living clean is not bondage; it is true freedom.

Again, let me emphasize the mandate to embrace the promise of purity found in Second Corinthians 7:1 *"Therefore, having these promises, beloved, let us cleanse ourselves from all filthiness of the flesh and spirit, perfecting holiness in the fear of God."* The results of this embrace will be our identification as sons and daughters of the Almighty

God. What an awesome motivation to strive for purity and avoid deception.

The Spirit of Truth is seeking to establish each one of us in truth. As Christ Jesus prayed to His Father, *"Sanctify them by Your truth; Your word is truth"* (John 17:17). As believers, we are to have upright lives that are characterized by authentic faith. Our walk must match our talk if we want our message to legitimately change lives. It is time for us to take a stand for righteousness and holiness. Grace is not a license for loose living.

In our attempts to appear politically correct, have we drifted far from the calling to stand for truth and righteousness? Only as we return to true holiness of heart can we be vessels of honor. This will allow us to be sanctified in truth and to be presentable to the Lord as consecrated vessels. The call is clear. We must walk in truth in order to powerfully present the Truth. And we must present the Truth in order to release freedom to reign in the hearts of people.

**Bobby Conner**

*Eagles View Ministries*

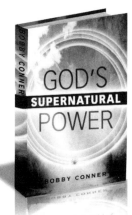

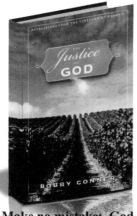